Beginning
BALLET

Joan Lawson

Beginning
BALLET

from the classroom to the stage

A & C Black · London
Theatre Arts Books/Routledge · New York

Paperback edition 1994. Reprinted 1996
First published 1977
A & C Black (Publishers) Limited
35 Bedford Row, London WC1R 4JH

ISBN 0-7136-3947-4

© 1994, 1958, 1972, 1977 A & C Black (Publishers)
Limited

Published simultaneously in U.S.A. by
Theatre Arts Books/Routledge
29 West 35th Street
New York City, NY 10001

ISBN 0-87830-056-2

Beginning Ballet comprises *Beginners, Please!* by the late
Kay Ambrose and *Dressing for the Ballet* by the late Peter
Revitt and Joan Lawson who has reworked some of the
material from both books. The original introduction by
Kay Ambrose has been slightly modified to take account
of prevailing practice.

CIP catalogue records for this book are avialable from
the British Library and the Library of Congress.

Typeset in 10 on 12pt Linotron Galliard by
Wyvern Typesetting Limited
Printed in Great Britain by Butler & Tanner Ltd,
Frome and London

Contents

Introduction

Dancing is something more than one of the arts – basically it is one of the instincts, and its history started long before there were any historians to write about it. Probably in its most ancient form it was ritualistic, but even then it must have been performed with conscious decorative intent. *Real* dancing is 'that dance which is as the very heartbeats of universal life' and, in the form of ballet, it is subject to all the rules which govern the great classical arts.

For instance, you cannot reasonably expect to become a great composer unless you study how to handle an orchestra, the various instruments, musical notation and the works of the great composers who have gone before you. To become a great painter you must study perspective, anatomy and architecture. A prospective poet must have a complete mastery of his language, an impeccable sense of rhythm and great visionary gifts. To become a great dancer you must have some, at least, of all these qualities, and the greatest dancers are the ones that have the most . . .

Dancing, music and painting are the three main components which make up ballet. Although to study music and painting is desirable for the prospective dancer, it is the first element, that of the basic technique of the classical ballet itself, which it is the hardest to establish. It is comparatively easy to lay down laws and precepts concerning musicians and painters, for we can always refer to great paintings and musical works to bear out what we want to say; but it is harder in the case of dancing! When the dancer has danced, the only thing which remains of the performance is the length of time it will live in the minds of those who saw it, unless, today, it is caught on film or video.

Luckily, however, a school of dancing is another matter, for it is concerned with an element which can lead to a generation of brilliant dancers – namely, the cultivation of an artistic standard, which can live, grow and develop for ever.

I wonder if there is anybody who has not at one time or another wondered what it would be like to float through the air like the immortal Pavlova, grip the imagination, like Nijinsky, dazzle like Fonteyn, with flawless technique, and play with the audience, like Nureyev? Indeed, to skim over the stage with sparkling footwork like a Collier, spin off-centre like a Baryshnikov or balance like a Guillem?

Some might comment 'What *fun!*' – disregarding the years of toil attached to these delightful powers.

Some might answer with a sigh, 'That would be a dream', and here, indeed, we have the more realistic approach of the two. The secret of the realisation of the dream is that *it must be a vision which can also be perceived by an audience.* Most of us have dreamed that we were flying, and sighed to remember the delicious and unearthly sensation the following morning, but Pavlova, who managed to keep her poetic interpretative powers unbruised by the drudgery of theatrical tours and the hard technical work of the classroom, was able to project the illusion of flying to those who saw her dance. Galina Ulanova achieved the same almost hypnotic power in Russia in her day.

So the first conscious realisation of ballet is in full accordance with the ancient belief that dancing must be a wholly unselfish art. A sentimental journey is no good in the theatre unless you can take your audience with you (after all, they have paid for their seats), and to watch a dancer who is enjoying herself in her own way, without reference to theatrical interpretation, is like watching a sleeper who

has a smile on her face, and wondering what she is dreaming about.

The first steps towards a sensitive and professional stage performance of ballet are the first steps of the student in the classroom, and it is with these preliminary movements that this little book is concerned.

FOR THE BEGINNER

My aim in writing has been to assemble the bare bones of elementary ballet (there is not room for any frills), and, of course, the difficulty has been to decide what material might safely be omitted. A more advanced book on ballet might well have been an easier task, as in that case one addresses students who one assumes are already acquainted with posture, and what to wear under their tights. It is not intended as a preparation for any particular examination in ballet, but is designed to be of practical assistance to boys and girls who wish to experiment gently at home before deciding to attend a ballet school, and for those who are attending classes, it may well serve them as a reference book and help them towards a better understanding of how their teacher is trying to train them. However, I hope sincerely that the number of ballet beginners who are unable to reach a class of any description will be few indeed.

In other words, although this book is not intended to take the place of a teacher of dancing it is an abbreviated primer. It gives a general idea of the sequence and purpose of a normal, preliminary ballet class, and it is also freely addressed to that army of ballet-lovers which forms the backbone of any audience, including photographers, artists, columnists and general connoisseurs.

The exercises shown here may seem rather dull, but as you will find they are surprisingly difficult; and if you master all the movements and poses and then perform them in the correct order the right number of times – i.e. if you 'do a class' lasting approximately an hour – you will certainly have achieved a good deal. As any dancer will tell you, doing a class on your own is difficult work even if you are already familiar with all the steps; however, do your best (working out the tempo will probably be the most awkward if you have no one to help you, although there are many good recordings of ballet class music available now), and when you do visit a ballet class you will not find yourself entirely lost.

TO THE TEACHER

Observe the average ballet class and then glance at the pictures of immortal dancers which usually decorate the studio walls. You are the person who has undertaken the miracle of turning one into the other, and this metamorphosis can take place only under your direct supervision, never from the pages of a book.

You will be the first to recognise the difficulties presented in compiling this small volume, where I have found myself thoroughly hedged in by a number of limitations, including lack of space. You must have found in the course of dance-training, part of which features the correction of faults in natural figure construction, that it is by a thousand subtle methods that you accustom the different dancers to master the difficult ballet technique and to recognise and respond to the different moods and timing of music, bearing in mind that some future choreographer may be using those same students to express his ballets. How can such subtleties be included in any book, let alone one of this size? The answer is, of course, that the subtleties of the dancer's training are entirely up to you.

The selection of steps, exercises and the drawings of basic poses shown here are adapted from a system which has proved to be a successful one, and which includes steps and information from various well-known methods of dancing.

For the information of the general reader, it must be strongly emphasised that a good teacher is always one who obtains excellent results from any system he or she has devised or adopted. A good system of dance-training – Cecchetti, Royal Academy of Dancing, Russian, etc. – is a good system no longer if indifferently taught.

FOR PARENTS AND GUARDIANS

For the parents of a really determined would-be dancer, ballet can be a grim subject. Most parents have no objection to a child taking ballet lessons as a part of a general education; but when the young person in question shows in no uncertain manner that he or she is absolutely resolved to take up professional ballet as a career, in very many cases some alarming problems present themselves. For instance, there is the awful uncertainty of height: for a girl, five foot six inches (1.68 metres) is the danger line. She must be prepared to start work seriously from the age of ten, or at the latest, twelve. Will she study ballet at the expense of some of her general education, and then grow too tall to make a first-rate dancer; or perhaps, suddenly lose interest?

At the very outset of this discussion one thing must be made clear. All uncertainties, including height, talent, strength and opportunities, are offset by one significant certainty – that whereas the serious study of ballet will bring increased poise and self-possession to the student, there is ample evidence that refusing to allow a determined child to study dancing will result in a very real frustration in later years, when it will be too late to cure.

As to the always vexed question, whether a child is really serious over a career in ballet or merely dazzled by films and star performances: an excellent test is to deliver a strong dose of ballet classes with a good teacher. As a rule, the teacher will be able to diagnose the seriousness and talent of the student; and anyway, the hard training for a ballet dancer will soon grow monotonous to any but the serious student, and will cure in record time someone who is merely stage-struck.

If the young dancer is firmly set on a training for a professional career, then there are three forms of funding involved. Scholarships are available which alleviate the high cost of a specialised training; in theory discretionary grants may be obtained from the student's local authority, although in practice this is becoming less and less likely as local councils struggle to meet their budgets; or the fees must be found privately.

Choice of teacher

This is a very serious matter indeed, as a mistake can be as far-reaching in its results as a wrong choice of medical advice. The best way of ensuring that a teacher is a reputable one is to communicate with one of the best known Teachers' Associations, which will be allied to one or more of the most famous and approved methods of dancing, some of which are referred to in these pages.

Parents should also bear in mind that endless displays and recitals by young students are not necessarily indicative of good ballet training. It may be suitable for those who wish to pursue the more commercial side of stage entertainment, but perpetual displays by tiny tots and young students should be regarded rather as an advertising campaign by a commercially minded teacher than as good experience for the pupils. One recital a year is quite enough for any teacher, mother or student: remember that the greatest teachers of dancing give a students' recital once in a blue moon, if ever. Once again, tradition has shown that premature stage appearances merely tend to make ballet pupils unduly conceited, and encourage the teacher to believe in his or her perfections as a 'choreographer' – a much misunderstood word, now used to describe the efforts of anyone who

attempts to arrange dances of any kind. So remember – although a ballet dancer must be good to be commercially successful, it does not work the other way round.

The danger of sending a child to a bad teacher cannot be overstressed. It is my painful duty to place on record that there are very many cases of children who, showing remarkable talent, have been allowed to study for some time with a bad teacher; the parents, at last discovering that the teacher was not *bona fide*, have taken the child away and sent it to a qualified teacher, but often too late. The second teacher has had the heartbreaking task of telling the parents that the child has been physically ruined, and can never be cured of the effects of a really shocking start.

Allowing a child to rise on her *pointes* before she is ready is one of the most outstanding examples of bad training; but there are a thousand physical maladjustments which may take place as a result of improper instruction – none of which would be noticed by any but an expert in its early stages. So be warned!

A qualified teacher is a person who can and should be approached on every matter concerning the serious student's welfare, including what sports and recreations may be studied without spoiling the ideal dancer's physique, and also upon the important question of shoes. There are a number of ballet shoe manufacturers producing *pointe* and soft shoes which have been developed for many years to help protect and strengthen the feet in the right way.

Whereas no trouble should be spared to find the right teacher for the prospective ballet student, many parents and guardians may be glad to have certain information before starting the search. I will therefore include a few basic facts which should be taken in the same spirit as the drawings of technical ballet steps which follow: they are addressed to those people who want to obtain a general idea of the subject before approaching an expert.

General information

Age and height

In the case of children who are under seven years of age, 'dancing classes' composed of little steps accompanied by nursery rhymes and other simple tunes are more suitable than ballet classes. Children under seven are not usually physically or mentally ready for rigorous ballet training, except in the most extraordinary cases.

At the age of twelve or thirteen a girl is usually considered too old to commence training and become a really excellent dancer. Nevertheless girls have been known who have started at fourteen and have made successful careers.

Boys are fundamentally stronger physically than girls and can start their training later, but they should not be older than fourteen if they are to make excellent dancers. However, it must be placed on record that one very famous dancer started his training at the age of twenty-two.

As to height: for girls, five foot six inches (1.68 metres) is the usual limit, but taller dancers have been known who have made extremely successful careers. In a young child, long hands and feet are danger signals, usually indicating height to come, but not invariably so.

Preliminary study

(The following information is exclusive of tiny tots and infant prodigies.)
a For a preliminary student, two one-hour classes a week constitute the average.
b During this class, *all* the exercises given in this book for the *barre* should be performed. (Naturally, a beginner would take some weeks at least to learn the movements, quite a time to grow accustomed to them and – in keeping with ballet as a whole – the rest of his life trying to perfect them!)
c Still in the course of that hour, in the second part of the class known as *centre practice*, separate attention should be given to the

exercises listed under that heading. It should be borne in mind that it is better to improve two exercises than to rush through too many steps imperfectly. Time should always be left for at least one *adage* and some *allegro* before the hour is over.

It should be noted that no student is expected to master all the steps shown in this book in his or her first few visits to the class-room. All the material shown is basic, and it may be mastered in the time specified by the teacher. The *pointe*-work shown is preliminary, but can only be attempted after training in soft practice shoes is complete and approved by the teacher. In fact –

d *No pointe-work should be attempted until at least two years of study are complete.*

It should then only take place under the guidance of a qualified teacher.

No child should be permitted to rise on her *pointes* until she has passed her tenth year. If she takes her first class when she is ten, she must under no circumstances try *pointe*-work until she is twelve, and so on.

e For parents who wish to know how much time is necessary to devote to ballet training for a child, say, of ten years who is to become a serious student with a view to a professional career, the approximate time of study would depend upon the type of school attended. Some professional schools for children from the age of eight upwards have already been set up and these, of necessity, have their own special time-tables in which a daily class in classical dance lasting from forty minutes to one hour finds a place together with the aver-age school syllabus. However, not all children can attend such schools. Instead they go to the numerous kinds of state-supported or independent schools and usually have to find time for dancing lessons elsewhere. If the child intends studying seriously then he or she should take at least two lessons a week, one after school and one on Saturday morn-ing. It is sometimes possible to increase the number of lessons to three a week, but this

depends greatly upon the amount of the child's homework and the travel entailed. Most children, however, find that even this is too much, particularly between the ages of fifteen to sixteen when they are working towards their G.C.S.E. exams. At sixteen it is a little late to begin serious study.

f Technical terms in ballet are mostly in French, and as part of every student's training naturally consists of ballet 'theory', these terms may present a stumbling block to some young people. There is little space in this book to pursue the derivations of the French terms, and none to arrange a system of phon-etic pronunciation: so I have indicated the approximate meanings only. For exact trans-lations and pronunciation the best course would be to secure a small French dictionary, which usually gives some general system for phonetic pronunciation in the introductory matter, and a ballet dictionary in which ballet terms can be found and identified.

The value of learning these French terms at the outset of one's ballet education is obvi-ous. Their use in training is international; so with their help one may study ballet coher-ently with a teacher in any country in the world – even if one does not understand the language used, outside the classroom.

g There are many uses for each step, position and movement, but partly from lack of space and partly to retain simplicity the main uses only are indicated.

No single method of dancing has been adhered to. The exercises are elementary, are an aggregate of various methods, and if care-fully followed will not impart to the students any tricks or habits which will render them unsuitable to continue training with any good teacher of ballet.

The technical terms used are those of the Cecchetti method, the system used by Miss Ambrose when she worked with Ballet Ram-bert and the National Ballet of Canada, both of which at that time used this firm basis for training their dancers.

BASIC COSTUME

Ballet shoes

As the ballet shoe is the most important tool for all dancers in the classroom and in Classical and Romantic ballet, its proper preparation and maintenance are vital.

Darning

Materials required
Large darning needles: the curved ones are most useful. Carpet thread or stranded cotton, the same colour as the shoe.

Method
The shoe, which is best made of satin, must be correctly fitted and, whether blocked or unblocked, should be darned before use to strengthen it and prolong its life. There are several methods of darning: the following is simple and effective.

1 Place shoe on foot and slightly soil the surface by turning the toe either on half-point (unblocked shoe) or full point (blocked shoe). This will indicate how far the darning must come up the satin. It should not be visible when the dancer is on her toes.

2 Starting as near as possible to the end of the leather sole, stitch a series of bars of three-stranded thread to and fro across the toe until they reach as far as indicated by soiling. Thrust needle well into satin: this is easier with a curved needle.

3 Again starting near the leather sole, blanket stitch over each set of three strands, linking these rows together by pushing needle through loops of rows below (**A**). Continue until all bars are covered (**B**).

Some dancers (usually those with narrow feet) require no further darning on their shoes. But if the satin at the side of the toe and under big and little toe joints shows signs of wear, these points should be darned as well.

Sewing on ribbons

Materials required
Amount of ribbon required depends on size of ankle. It should be no less than $\frac{1}{2}$ in. (1.5cm) wide and long enough to cross twice in front and twice behind ankle, as well as allowing some for knot. 2–2¼ yd (2m) is usually enough. Tape to same length if required.

Method
1 Fit shoe on foot and adjust drawstring, knotting this securely when it is sufficiently tight to hold shoe comfortably on foot (**C**).

2 Fold back seam straight forwards towards inside sole. Ribbons must be sewn where fold of shoe comes at either side. They should be sewn with raw edge well turned in on inside

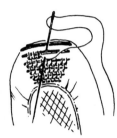

A method of darning

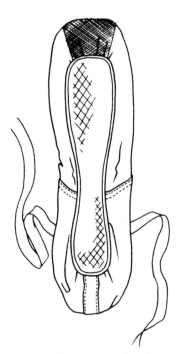

B darning completed

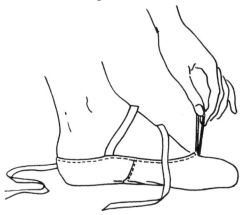

C adjust drawstring

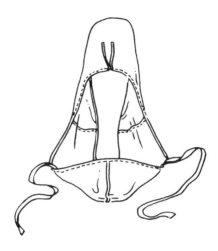

D fold back seam flat

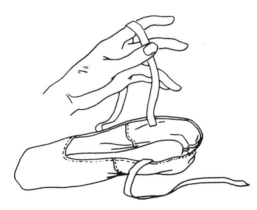

E tilt ribbons forwards

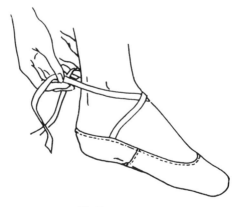

F first cross

of shoe and must tilt slightly forwards so that they will fit flat over instep. Ribbons must be hemmed on securely and no knot should be used as this irritates and bruises the flesh (**D**, **E**).

3 If a strong ribbon with non-slippery back is used (which is usually the case in the USA) it need not be strengthened. But if a thin or very slippery ribbon is used it must be strengthened with tape or it will not grip. Tape is a little narrower than ribbon. It is sewn on after ribbon has been attached and is lightly caught on ribbon itself.

Some dancers prefer tape to be as long as ribbon. Others prefer a short piece stretching as far as first crossing of both ribbons at back of ankle. They then add another short piece of tape where knot is tied.

Tying the shoe

The shoe must be tied with foot flat on floor, and the leg leaning slightly backwards. It must never be tied with toe on full or half-point as this allows no flexibility of the ankle and prevents a full movement of the foot in *demi-* and full *pliés*.

1 Bring both ribbons forwards, cross them and allow them to lie flat on centre front of foot roughly at level of ankle bones (**F**).

2 Take both ribbons round to back of ankle. They must lie above ankle bones and cross one on top of the other at centre back of leg (**G**).

3 Bring both ribbons forwards, crossing them one on top of the other so that they lie flat at centre front of leg and a little higher than first crossing (**H**).

4 Take both ribbons to back and knot them on outside of leg between ankle bone and Achilles tendon. They must be knotted twice and the loose ends pushed down this slight hollow and underneath the ribbons so that no ends are visible (**I**).

If the knot is tied on the outside of the leg there is less danger of the knot being rubbed

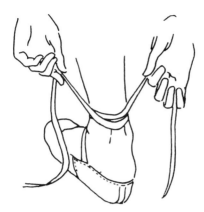

G second cross

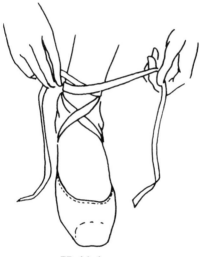

H third cross

I tuck in loose ends

undone against the opposite leg in *batterie*, etc.

Some dancers have difficulty in keeping on their shoes, in which case a piece of elastic long enough to go round the ankle may be sewn with both ends to the back seam of the shoe. The elastic is drawn round the ankle before ribbons are tied. If, however, the shoe is properly fitted when bought, this should not be necessary.

It is never advisable to use a loop of elastic at the back seam and to slip the ribbons through this as the action of the foot is impeded because the ribbons do not hold the shoe properly.

Maintenance

Never throw old shoes away without preserving the inner sole (**J**), the leather piece reinforcing the instep (**K**), and the dolly (**L**), i.e. the piece reinforcing the block, if these are unbroken. They can all be used to reinforce shoes when they soften. The most important piece is that reinforcing the block, as this part of the shoe deteriorates more rapidly than any other.

To reinforce the back

1 Raise inner sole, being careful not to break it. If it is tacked down, remove tacks first before levering it upwards with table knife.
2 Remove all superfluous matter from old back (e.g. old glue). If it seems thick, pare off some of the leather at the top end. Cover with glue or suitable brand adhesive and stick directly on top of back still on shoe. Press firmly, being careful not to press it further into toe than indicated by back still in shoe.
3 Glue in inner sole, pressing this firmly and again not allowing it to slip upwards into toe.
4 Stuff toe with soft cloth, place a weight inside shoe and allow to harden before wearing.

The same process can be used if instep piece or inner sole weakens. When these pieces crack or break they should be removed and replaced by whole pieces. It is rarely advisable to have more than one of these pieces in the shoe at a time, unless they are very thin, and never when they are broken.

Re-blocking the toe

This is best done by pouring some liquid shellac into the toepiece and rolling it carefully round inside the block until it soaks the canvas. Be careful to leave no superfluous drops anywhere as these harden and press into the foot. Once shellac has soaked in, leave shoe to harden for at least twelve hours.

Liquid shellac is easily made by shaking powdered shellac with methylated spirits until it dissolves. But it can usually be bought ready mixed from paint and hardware stores.

Cleaning shoes

Shoes must be kept clean and this is best done with benzine or surgical spirit. Dip an old toothbrush into the benzine and brush soiled parts of shoes. If this is done frequently the dirt will not grind into the satin.

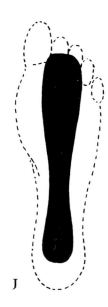

J

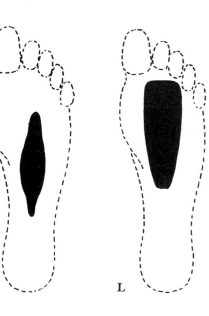

K   L

Hair-dressing

The hair for all Classical and Romantic ballet should be parted in the centre so that the movements of the head may appear to be as equally balanced as those of the limbs. It must be worn close to the head. This practice should be started in the classroom. It is usual to dress the hair as tightly as possible. If it is short, it should be securely pinned into a net. If long, it should be braided and worn over the top of the head or twisted into a bun and pinned into a net. Over the net is worn a band of net or ribbon.

For pupils and young students it is advisable to wear the hair well above the nape of the neck to ensure freedom for all head movements, with band tied in front. (*Top left*)

For students and professionals some licence can be taken and the band worn tied behind, and the hair perhaps lower. (*Top centre*)

For boys it is quite useful to wear a sweat band. (*Top right*)

For Romantic ballet there is a clearly recognised style. The hair is pulled over the ears and drawn backwards into a low coil or bun. (*Bottom left*)

For National dance the hair is worn more freely – often in plaits laced with ribbon. (*Bottom right*)

Dress for the classroom and stage

It is essential that the dancer at all times appears neat and appropriately dressed, particularly so in the classroom where every movement must be seen by the teacher and not hidden by bunches of material, untidy hair or baggy tights. It is in the classroom that pupil and student first learn the need for discipline in dress. Garments must be simple and easy to keep clean. The traditional wear for girls is tunic or leotard with footless knitted tights, cotton socks and crossover; for boys footless tights, cotton socks and singlet or shirt.*

Stage costumes have to be made for the end of the year and other shows and the first essential of any costume is that it should fit exactly and be comfortable. For this reason every garment must be made to fit the individual for whom it is intended. The measuring chart (pages 18–19) is meant as a guide to be followed when cutting and making any garment drawn in this book. If the measurements (indicated by figures) and points (indicated by letters) are carefully taken and marked, it is simple to draw the outline of each garment for the paper pattern which should always be made before cutting the material.

There are certain peculiarities to be observed when making costumes for dancing, particularly those for Classical, Romantic and *demi-caractère* ballet.

Length

Extra length should always be allowed at the waist for the rise and fall of the chest when the dancer stretches and raises the arms. This is particularly important in male costumes when lifts are to be performed.

*These garments have been largely superseded by commercially produced leotards and tights but they are seldom all-cotton and will not always fit well.

Armholes and sleeves

Allow the armholes of any garment with sleeves to fit as high into the armpit and shoulder as possible. The sleeve is therefore always set higher on bodice or shirt than in normal dress. The bodice must be tightly fitting and if the design requires that the bodice should look loose or be draped it is better to set the sleeve on a tight-fitting lining.

Backing material

It is always better to back material rather than line it, particularly if the garment is to be tight-fitting.** Never skimp material as turnings must always be firm.

Use stiff material with care as it is rarely suitable for anything but certain period costumes; the court robes in *The Sleeping Beauty* could well be made of heavy brocade or velvet.

Fitting

Always fit any off-the-shoulder garment carefully so that it will not impede the dancer's movement. It is often best in such cases to make a firm tutu-like bodice which fits exactly, and then set another bodice cut to the necessary shape over this. Or make the off-the-shoulder effect with soft draperies caught on a high, tight-fitting bodice of net.

Always test the hang of draperies and set of sleeves, collars, skirts, etc., by watching the dancer in movement. Dance movement should never be impeded or hidden by costume, or by additions to costume, except in those cases where historical fashion has to be followed exactly.

**Bolton sheeting and calico are still used by professional makers of dance costumes but both are difficult to obtain. They can be replaced by firm, closely woven cotton cloth such as heavy poplin.

Making patterns

Colour

Colour in stage costume must always be considered. It often loses effectiveness the moment stage lighting is brought into play. Whites, creams, pinks, reds, and all kinds of yellow and black are usually safe in any circumstances. Blues, greens, mauves or purples, and browns can easily become grey unless the producer fully understands how to use the correct lighting to maintain the original tints.

When making use of the pattern diagrams given, readers are advised to make out their own patterns according to measurements given by the dotted lines. The thick inner line marks the actual place for machining or stitching hem or seam. This has been done so that allowance can be made for turnings and for adjustments that may be necessary to suit an individual.

Always allow at least $\frac{3}{4}$ in. (2cm) for turnings as seams in dancing costumes must be firm and properly finished.

Unless otherwise stated, width of materials used is 35–36 in. (90cm).

In order to facilitate the making of an outline each pattern has been drawn on squared paper. For bust measurements from 30–32 in., each square should represent $\frac{3}{4}$ in. (2cm); from 32–34 in., the square should measure $\frac{7}{8}$ in. (2.25cm); and from 34–36 in. the square should measure 1 in. (2.5cm). But it cannot be emphasised strongly enough that each garment must be fitted to the individual before it is finally sewn together.

Note The measurements in this book are first given in inches. One inch is 2.54 centimetres. So to convert the inches to centimetres, multiply them by 2.54.

For example,
15 inches = 15 × 2.54 centimetres
= 38.1 centimetres.

A rough and ready conversion for small numbers of inches is to multiply them by 5 and divide by 2.

For example,
12 inches = $\dfrac{12 \times 5}{2}$ = 30 centimetres

MEASURING CHART FOR CUTTING A PATTERN

Note Front and back markings are similar but measurements are not identical; these parts must therefore be marked and cut out separately.

POINTS TO BE MARKED

a shoulder point
b centre neck
c crutch
d underarm
e where bust line ends at side seam
f hip joint
g knee
h ankle
j centre waist front
k centre waist back
l top of leg back

MEASUREMENTS

Bust (widest part)
Waist
Hips (widest part)
Shoulder to crutch
Shoulder to waist
Centre underarm to waist
Underarm from **d** to elbow or wrist
Crutch to knee and ankle

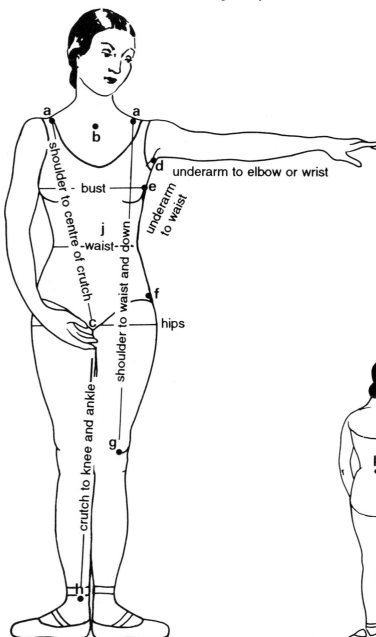

HOW TO CUT A PATTERN

1 Mark a line down centre of material. This will represent centre body line either front or back. It must run parallel to selvedges unless otherwise indicated in drawings.

2 On this line measure length from **c** (crutch) to **b** (centre neck) marking these points and point **j** (centre waist at the front) or point **k** (centre waist at the back). Point **b** must be at least 2½in. (6.5cm) from edge of material.

3 Measure and mark waistline, being careful that this lies at right angles to centre line. It will be subject to adjustment, particularly if tucks are to be made underarm. In the case of a fitted garment this line must end exactly under point **d** where the side seam will be. (Do not mark **d** yet.)

4 Measure and mark a line from waist to shoulder parallel to centre line and mark point **a** on both sides of centre line. Test the accuracy of this line by measuring a diagonal line from point **a** to **c** (crutch). Point **a** must be vertically above fullest point of bust.

In the case of fitted garments both these lines help to indicate the shaping at the waist both upwards and downwards, as darts can be made on either line.

5 Measure widest part of bust or torso and mark this line, being careful that measurements from points **a** and **b** are correct. Also measure from this line upwards to point **d** and mark this. It should indicate proper depth of armhole.

Bust line must end exactly under **d** at point **e** which will indicate position of seam. In a feminine fitted garment this point and line will indicate shaping of bodice on bust line.

6 Measure length of shoulder line from **a** towards arm. This should slope at an angle of 80 degrees to line drawn from **a** to waist. But this slope must be adjusted to individual requirements. Similarly length of shoulder seam will be determined by shape of garment, e.g. a sleeved blouse may require 5 in. (12.5cm), whilst a practice tunic may only

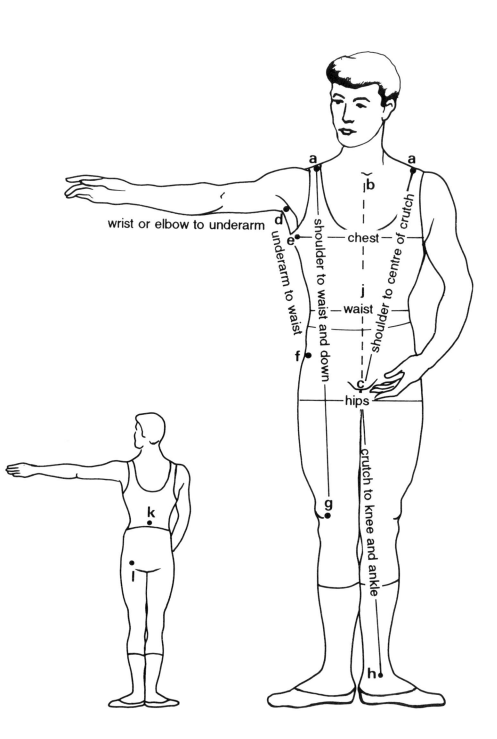

need to continue downwards for 3 in. (7.5cm) from **a**.

7 If sleeves are required, measurements should be taken from point **d** to elbow or wrist, or to point required by design. It is also useful to measure from end of shoulder seam down the top of the arm to length required.

8 Measure round widest part of hips. Mark this line carefully, noting its correct distance from waistline downwards and from crutch upwards to where this line crosses centre of material.

For all fitted garments this line should end directly under point **d**, in the same way as bust and waistlines.

9 To determine length of tunic, shirt or blouse, and any type of garment falling from shoulders, measure carefully through line commencing at **a** straight downwards and from **b** to crutch and downwards, continuing until requisite length is reached.

10 For garments suspended from waist, such as short knickers or leotards, it is most valuable to mark point **f** at hip joint. This is best found if the dancer raises the body well upwards from the waist and bends straight forwards. A curved line drawn from **c** to **f** and slightly downwards again to side seam will give contour of front of garment. For back of garment, a measurement should be made from waist downwards over broadest part of hip to top of leg whilst dancer is bending. A curve is then drawn from **c** downwards to point **l** and then upwards to side seams.

11 For tights and long trousers, measure from crutch to knee (point **g**) and on to ankle bone (point **h**). This measurement should be made without any turning-out of the legs.

12 Tights will also require measurements of ankle, calf and thigh.

Knitwear

Abbreviations for all knitting instructions
st – stitch(es)   no. – number   K – knit
P – purl   st.st – stocking (US stockinette)
stitch (K row, P row)   inc. – increase
dec. – decrease   tog. – together   fol. –
following   beg. – beginning   cast off = US
bind off

THE FOOTLESS TIGHTS

Tights knitted on four needles are more comfortable as the shaping appears in the correct
place at the back of the leg and there is no
side seam to rub the ankle. They are also more
economical in wool. (The patterns can however be knitted on two needles if preferred.)
Individual measurements must be carefully
taken. (See pages 18–19.)

Materials required
Amount of wool depends entirely on size and
ranges from 5oz (125g) for a child to 8oz
(225g) for larger sizes. A set or pair of 2 mm
(old UK 12; US 2) needles and a set or pair
of 3 mm (old UK 9; US 5) needles. Use 3-ply
wool.

Tension (US: gauge)
7 st and 9 rows to 1 in. using 3 mm needles.

Method
Measure ankle and multiply no. of inches by
7, adding 2 st for every extra $\frac{1}{4}$ in., e.g. for
8 in. ankle, 56 st are required; for $8\frac{1}{4}$ in., 58
st; $8\frac{1}{2}$ in., 60 st, etc. Using set of 2 mm
needles, cast on loosely requisite no. of st,
dividing them equally over 3 needles. Work
in K1, P1 rib for $1\frac{1}{2}$ in. (small sizes) or 2
in. (larger sizes).

Change to set of 3 mm needles and work
in st.st (**NB** if using 4 needles K each round).

Inc. at beg. of first and in last but one st of
3rd needle in the 14th and every fol. 14th
row until work measures length from ankle
to knee (i.e. increase every $1\frac{1}{2}$ in.).

Continue as above but inc. at beg. of first
and in last but one st of 3rd needle in the 9th
and every fol. 9th row (i.e. every 1 in.) until
work measures $1\frac{1}{2}$in. longer than measurement from crutch to ankle measured on
straight of knitting.

Divide for crutch and top of right leg K quarter
total no. of st (e.g. if there are 96 st on
needles, K24), turn and P to end (i.e. across
all 96 st).

Continue in st.st, increasing at each end of
needles for next 6 rows (hips below 30 in.);
8 rows (hips 30–34 in.); 10 rows (hips 34–
36 in.); 12 rows (hips over 36 in.).

Work 4 rows without shaping.

K2 tog. at each end of next and every fol.
4 rows 6 times. Continue knitting 2 tog.
every 4th row at back of tights only, until
front measures length from waist to crutch
measured on straight of knitting.

Shape for back 1st row – P to last 14 st (small
sizes); 16 st (hips 30–34 in.); 18 st (hips over
34 in.). Turn and K back.
2nd row – P to last 28 st. Turn and K back.
Continue in this way purling 10 st less each
row until none remains. Change to 2 mm
needles and rib K1 P1 across all st for 2 in.,
or until leg is sufficient length from waist to
crutch to allow it to be turned over belt. Cast
off.

Knit left leg in same manner until dividing
for crutch. Here K across $\frac{3}{4}$ amount of st
(e.g. if 96 st on needles, K 72, turn and P
back). Then continue as above. Dec. at one
end of needle for back shaping, and at other
end of needle for waist shaping.

Gusset Using a pair of 3 mm needles, cast on 2 st, P back. Continue in st.st, increasing at each end of needle every other row until there are 14 st on needle (hips below 30 in.); 18 st (hips 30–34 in.); 22 st (hips 34–36 in.); 26 st (hips over 36 in.). Work 2 rows, then dec. at each end of needle every other row until 2 remain. Cast off.

Stitch up back and front seams and insert gusset as in drawing, taking care to stitch the cast-on and cast-off st at lower end of front and back seams. Press lightly.

Methods for keeping up tights

There are several ways for keeping up tights. Footless tights are often kept up with a belt (**A**) by both girl and boy. Or a piece of elastic can be run through top. Other methods for woven tights of silk, nylon or cotton are:

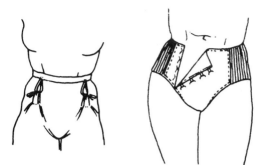

B with elastic and tape   **C** with jock-strap

For girls
1 Pieces of wide elastic to fit waist on which are sewn four pieces of tape with double ends. Four loops of elastic or elastic and tape are sewn on tights at points 1 in. above **f** (see page 18) at back and front of tights. These are lined and tied (**B**).
2 By a jock-strap (**C**), which should be opened at one side, bound with tape after which strong hooks and eyes must be sewn on as for a tutu basque (see page 63).

For boys
1 By elastic bands worn over shoulders at point **a** (see page 19). These cross each other and are caught at centre back – no higher (**D**).
2 By turning tights over a belt and securing firmly.

A knitted tights with belt

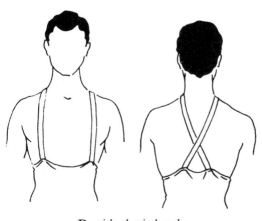

D with elastic bands

THE CROSSOVER (ADULT)

Materials required

Amount of wool depends entirely on size and ranges from 4oz (125g) for a child to 6oz (175g) for large sizes. Pair of 2 mm (old UK 12; US 2) needles and a pair of 3 mm (old UK 9; US 5) needles. Use 3-ply wool.

Tension (US: gauge)

7 st and 9 rows to 1 in. on 3 mm needles.

Back

3 sizes (larger sizes in brackets)

Using 2 mm needles cast on 94 st (32–34 in. bust); 100 st (34–36 in. bust); 106 st (36–38 in. bust). Rib K1 P1 for 2½ in. (small size) and 3 in. (larger sizes).

Change to 3 mm needles and st.st. Inc. at each end of 9th and every fol. 9th row until there are 108 (114, 120) st on needle. Continue until work measures requisite length from armhole to waist, allowing at least 1 in. extra if the dancer wishes her crossover to fit snugly round the waistline whilst in movement.

Armhole Cast off 6 (7, 8) st at beg. of next 2 rows. K2 tog. at both ends of every other row until 84 (90, 96) st remain. Continue in st.st. until work measures 6½ in. (6¾ in., 7 in.) from beg. of armhole.

For shoulder Cast off 9 (10, 11) st at beg. of next 2 rows 3 times in all. Cast off remaining stitches.

Right front

Using 2 mm needles cast on 87 (93, 96) st. Rib K1 P1 for 2½ in. (small size) and 3 in. (larger sizes).

Change to 3 mm needles and leaving a border of 9 st in K1 P1 rib, change to st.st, knitting 2 tog. inside ribbing on 3rd and every fol. 3rd row. At same time, inc. 1 st at other end of every 9th row until there are 72 (78, 84) st on needle and work measures same as back as far as armhole.

Adult crossover

Armhole Continue to K2 tog. inside rib on every 3rd row, but cast off 7 (8, 9) st on next 2 rows, then K2 tog. at armhole end of every other row 6 (7, 8) times.

Continue knitting 2 tog. inside ribbing until there are 36 (39, 42) st on needle and work measures same as back from armhole to shoulder.

For shoulder Cast off 9 (10, 11) st at beg. of next and every alternate row 3 times. On next row K2 tog. then continue in K1 P1 rib on remaining 9 st for 1 in. for strip round back of neck.

Left front

Knit as for right front reversing the shapings.

Sleeve

Using 2 mm needles cast on 66 (70, 74) st. Rib K1 P1 for 1½ in. Change to 3 mm needles and st.st. Inc. 1 st at each end of every 3rd row until there are 84 (90, 94) st on needle and work measures 5 in. (5½ in., 6 in.) measured on straight.

Shaping top of sleeve K2 tog. at each end of every alternate row until there are 56 (60, 64) st. Now K2 tog. at each end of every row until there are 16 (20, 24) st. Cast off.

Knit another sleeve to match.

Tie
Using 3 mm needles cast on 16 st and knit a strip in K1 P1 rib measuring at least 15 in.
Knit another strip in same way.

Make-up
Press all pieces lightly, avoiding ribbing.
Stitch side seams together leaving right side open ½in. from lower edge to top of rib. (This opening is for tie.) Seam shoulders and strap at back of neck. Seam sleeves and set in armhole. Sew ties to fronts.

CHILDREN'S CROSSOVERS (THREE SIZES)

These are knitted as those for adult but without side shapings. Use same needles: 2 mm for ribbing at waist and bottom edge of sleeve, 3 mm for st.st.

Back
Cast on 78 (26 in. bust), 84 (28 in. bust), 90 (30 in. bust), rib for 2 in., then change to st.st and continue straight until armhole is reached.

Armhole Cast off 4 (5, 5) st on next 2 rows then K2 tog. at each end of every alternate row 4 (5, 5) times. Continue till work measures 5¾ in. (6 in., 6¼ in.). Cast off 7 (8, 8) st at beg. of next 2 rows, 3 times in all. Cast off.

Fronts
Cast on 75 (80, 86) st; rib 2 in. Change to st.st and leaving rib of 9 st, K2 tog. inside ribbing on every 3rd row right up to shoulder. K straight at side until armhole is reached. Cast off 5 st (all sizes) on next row. Then K2 tog. at armhole end on every alternate row 4 (5, 5) times. Knit till work measures same as back. Cast off 7 (8, 8) st at armhole end on the next alternate 3 rows. Rib at least 9 st for 1 in. (1¼ in., 1¼ in.). Cast off.

Sleeves
Using 2 mm needles, cast on 56 (60, 64) st. Rib K1 P1 for 1 in. Change to 3 mm needles and st.st. Increase at each end of every 3rd row until there are 70 (74, 78) st and work measures 4 in. (4¼ in., 4¾ in.). K2 tog. at each end of needle on every alternate row until 40 (44, 48) st remain. Then K2 tog. at each end of every row until 16 (18, 20) st remain. Cast off.

Tie
Knit same as for adults.

Make-up
As for adults.

CLASS

Preliminary notes

Before the pupil and student enter the classroom they will have understood the need for discipline in dress and simple hair-dos which are easy to keep clean. Since few alterations are made to classroom dress throughout their career, ballet students can forget their clothes on entering the classroom and learn the more difficult art of self-discipline and the basic rules of classical dance. At all times they must hold their bodies correctly and respond to the call of the music so that their movements are fully co-ordinated.

The basic rules can be roughly summarised thus:
1 The best results are obtained when the spine is stretched to its straightest but not stiffened.
2 The weight must always be carried forwards and a straight line be seen to run through each leg, when it is turned out, from the hip joint through the centre of each knee and foot.
3 The arms must never cross the centre line of the body nor go behind the shoulders.
4 The head must be held erect and freely poised with the eyes correctly focused at all times.

THE BARRE

The *barre* is usually to be found round the walls of a classroom, and is about 3 ft 6 in. (105 cm) from the floor. There are sometimes other *barres* of various heights underneath, suitable for younger performers. At home, a chair back is a good substitute for a *barre*; if you place too much pressure on it it will simply overbalance, and you with it.

Exercises for the *barre*, performed in the order given on page 28, are the correct and scientific way of warming up the body, loosening the joints and setting the circulation in motion before centre practice takes place. Each exercise should be performed the number of times indicated.

'Limbering' – stretching, kicking, etc. – is very dangerous until the body is 'warmed up' by *barre* exercises. Warmth in this sense has nothing to do with the weather.

Careful study of the drawings will show that the *barre* exercises contain bits of the more showy and glamorous exercises given later for centre practice.

The instructions given with each series of drawings have been kept to an absolute minimum on account of space.

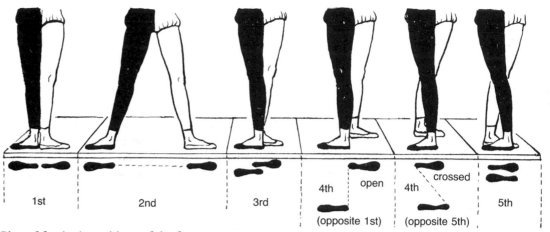

Plan of five basic positions of the feet

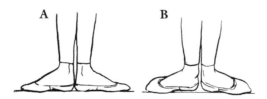

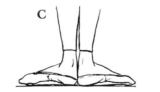

A well-placed feet and ankles.
B ankles are rolling and weight is on big toe.
C back view of **B**, showing how toes are cramped.

THE FIVE BASIC POSITIONS OF THE FEET

The five basic positions should be memorised in the first instance by the prospective dancer as training cannot begin without them. In all positions the feet should be turned out from the hip as this gives greater freedom for all types of movement. Beginners should not force their legs to turn out too greatly at first, as this usually results in rolling ankles. All the toes should be flat on the floor. If, for example, too much weight is taken on the big toe, the arch of the foot will be seen to flatten, which weakens the instep. In all positions when the heels are flat on the ground, the weight of the body should be shared equally by both legs.

If you have not paid attention to the correct placing of the feet on the floor, drawings **B** and **C** show how you may damage your feet.

Barre

BASIC DEPORTMENT

The correct distribution of the weight of the body is dependent on right posture at the *barre*.

1 shows the ideal posture – straight knees, all muscles pulled upwards so that the body has a slim line, and the hand resting lightly on the *barre*. Care should be taken not to place the hand too far back on the *barre* as this twists the shoulder.

2 is an example of the way height distribution is controlled when shifting from one position to another.

3a shows a foot half stretched, **3b** three quarters stretched, **3c** fully stretched, **3d** *sur la pointe*.

Before attempting any exercise care should be taken to ensure that the posture is correct (according to instructions on this page). The free arm (in this case, the right one) should have the elbow lifted and not be allowed to hug the side of the waist. The outside of the little finger should not be allowed to touch the front of the thigh but be about two to four inches (5–10 cm) away.

During the time devoted to assuming the correct posture the mind should also be schooled so that the exercise is performed intelligently and consciously. In other words – think what you are doing.

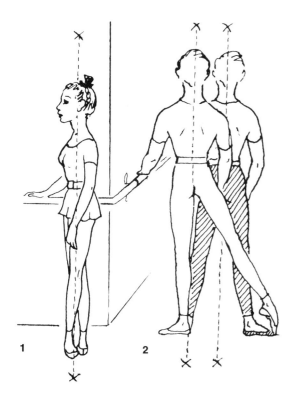
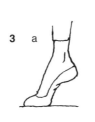

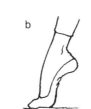
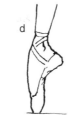

shift weight
of body as
toe moves

start here

1 *en première* (1st position)
2 *plié en première*
3 *en première* (repeat **1**)
4 *tendu à la seconde*
5 *en seconde* (2nd position)
6 *plié en seconde*
7 *en seconde*
8 *tendu à la seconde*
9 *en troisième* (3rd position)
10 *plié en troisième*
11 *en troisième* (repeat **9**)

Pliés at the barre in all positions of the feet

'*Plié*' is from the French verb *plier*, to bend. One of the main purposes of the exercise is flexibility of the knees. If these are held well back, the hip joints are loosened and the muscles of the groin stretched (which is already an aid to achieving a good 'turn out'

of the whole leg). Illustrations show erect figures in the basic positions of the feet and a full *plié* in each one. Sinking to the lowest point in a *plié* the student should pass through the quarter and *demi-plié* positions indicated in the sequence shown. As an exercise, two *pliés* should be executed in each position, using two bars of slow waltz time to go down, and two to come up. The change from

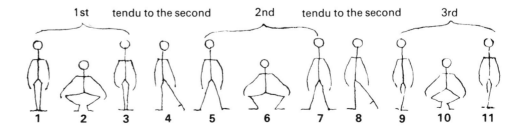

1st   tendu to the second   2nd   tendu to the second   3rd

1   2   3   4   5   6   7   8   9   10   11

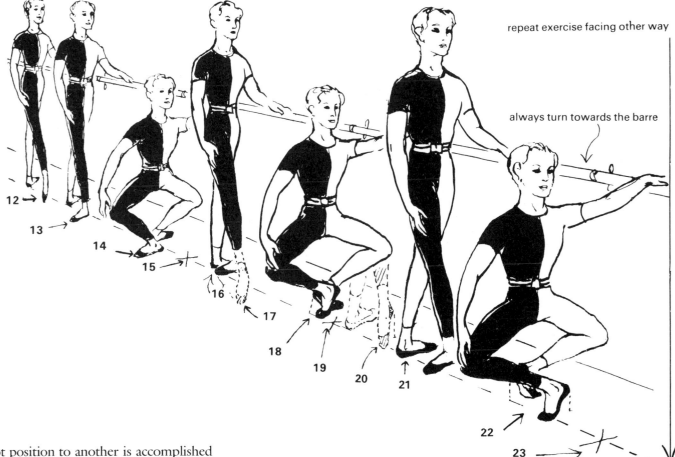

repeat exercise facing other way

always turn towards the barre

one foot position to another is accomplished by means of a (*battement*) *tendu*, as also shown by the sequence of pin-men below.

The *tendu* to the next position is taken quickly so that the student can start the next *plié* on the first beat of the bar. When the exercise is finished with the right leg, turn round and repeat it the other way.

At all times the back must be held erect.

12 *tendu à la quatrième: ouverte*
13 *en quatrième: ouverte* (4th position: open)
14 *plié en quatrième: ouverte*
15 *en quatrième: ouverte* (repeat **13**)
16 *tendu à la quatrième: ouverte*
17 *en cinquième* (5th position)
18 *plié en cinquième*
19 *en cinquième* (repeat **17**)
20 *tendu à la quatrième devant: croisée*
21 *en quatrième: croisée* (4th position: crossed)
22 *plié en quatrième: croisée*
23 *en quatrième: croisée* (repeat **21**)

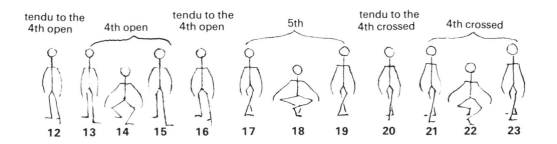

tendu to the 4th open   4th open   tendu to the 4th open   5th   tendu to the 4th crossed   4th crossed

12   13   14   15   16   17   18   19   20   21   22   23

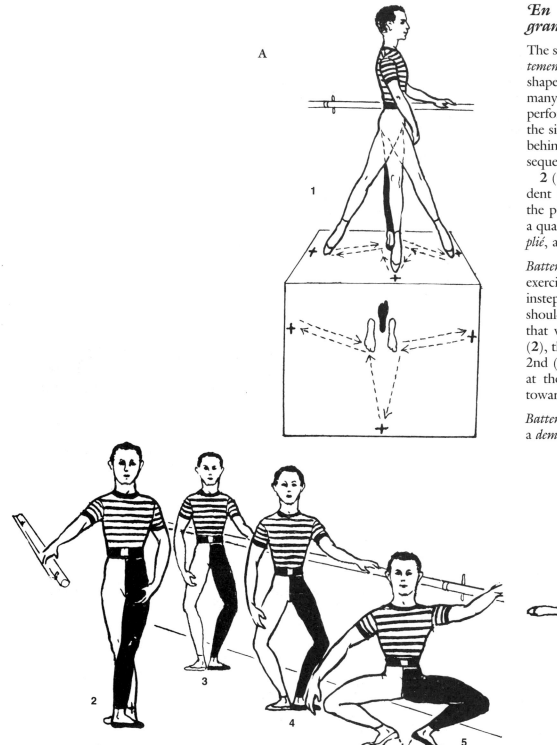

A

1

2 3 4 5 6

'En croix': battements tendus and grands battements

The sequence **A** here shows a man doing *battements tendus en croix*. 'En croix' means 'in the shape of a cross' and the term can apply to many exercises. An exercise *en croix* is always performed thus: to the front, closing front; to the side, closing behind; to the back, closing behind; to the side, closing front (see also sequence at top of facing page).

2 (below) shows the front view of the student standing in 5th position at the *barre*, the preliminary for many exercises. **3** shows a quarter *plié*, **4** a demi- (or half) *plié*, **5** a full *plié*, all in the first position of the feet.

Battements tendus. The main purpose of the exercise (**B**) is to stretch and strengthen the insteps. In the execution, the whole leg should be turned outwards from the thigh so that when the working foot is in 4th front (**2**), the heel is forced upwards; to the side in 2nd (**4**), the heel is forced forwards; in 4th, at the back (**6**), the heel is pushed down towards the ground.

Battements tendus can also be performed with a *demi-plié* in the closed positions.

B

Battements tendus

Battements tendus with a demi-plié

Grands battements. The instructions (**C**) for *battements tendus* also apply to *grands battements*, which are the throwing up of a straight leg, beginning and ending with a *tendu* as sketched. They are performed *en croix*, and can be done four times in each direction to begin with, and eight times as the pupil progresses. The purpose is to promote a general circulation of blood through the legs and to loosen the hip joints.

Battements tendus are usually performed to crisp 4/4 time, *en croix* 4 times with each leg (i.e. facing each way). 4/4 time also goes for *grands battements*, but played a little more slowly than for the *tendus*.

C

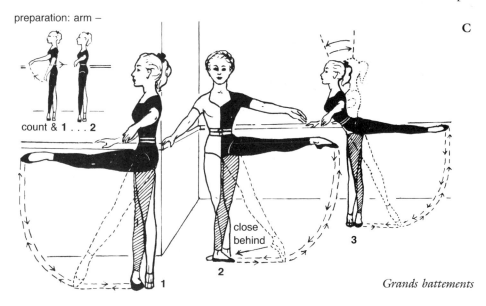

preparation: arm –

count & **1** **2**

close behind

Grands battements

A1-4: preparation for *ronds de jambe à terre en dehors*

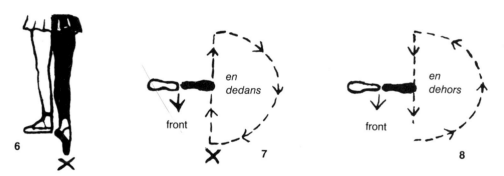

Ronds de jambe, à terre and en l'air; battements frappés and sur le cou de pied

Ronds de jambe à terre ('rounds with the leg on the ground'), *en dehors* (outwards) and *en dedans* (inwards) are exercises to loosen the hip joint. They are always done outwards first (**A5** and **8**) and are performed in a slow 3/4 time. On the first beat of the bar the heels are always together in 1st position. The working leg should move smoothly and continuously when the exercise has been learned, but a good method for the absolute beginner is to do the 'round' in four stages, i.e. in slow motion, using a whole bar for each movement. Do eight *ronds de jambe* each way with each leg.

Battements frappés ('knocked beats') are for strengthening and developing the instep, and also serve to increase the ultimate elevation of the student. When the heel of the working leg is placed on either side of the ankle of the supporting leg (**B2** and **4**) the foot should be relaxed as shown. **3** and **5** show the working foot extending sharply to the 2nd position, hitting the floor as it goes (hence the 'knock').

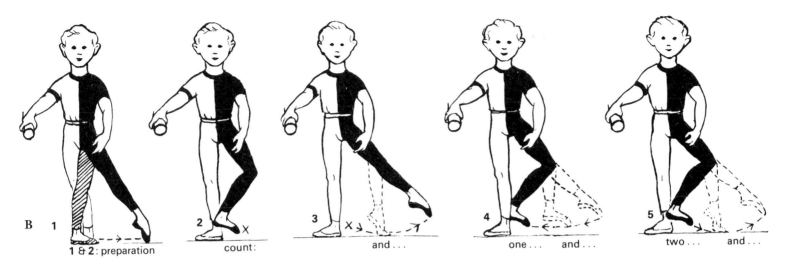

B 1

1 & 2: preparation

2 count:

3 and . . .

4 one . . . and . . .

5 two . . . and . . .

When thus extended (**3**) the toe should not be more than two inches (5 cm) off the ground. Exercise: 16 counts with each leg.

Battements sur le cou de pied ('beats on the neck of the foot'). This exercise is a preparation for future *batterie* (part of advanced steps such as *brisés* and *entrechats*). At first the movement (**C2 to 4**) should be practised very slowly with equal accent both when the feet are together and apart; then it should be practised in double time and the speed should be gradually increased as the pupil becomes more adept.

Practise for **32** counts with each leg, and increase after the first few months.

Battements sur le cou de pied sur la demi-pointe ('on half point'). This movement is exactly the same as the previous one but the instep of the working foot is fully stretched, as shown in illustration **C5**, and the supporting foot on half point throughout. Do not allow the body to sway and wobble, and do not attempt this exercise until you have mastered the previous one.

16 counts for each leg.

C

1

preparation as in **b**
preliminary position for
battements sur-le-cou-de-pied

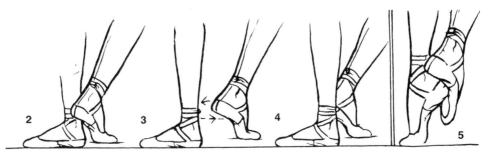

2

3

4

5

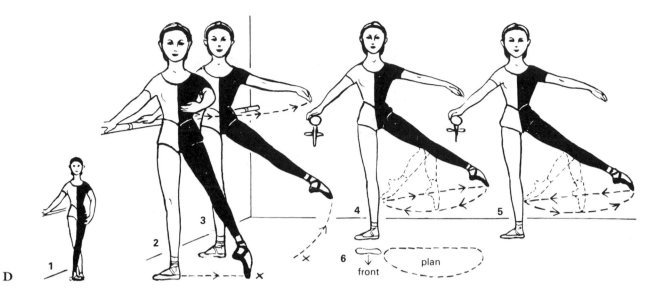

D

Ronds de jambe en l'air ('in the air'). This helps flexibility of the knee joint and aids the turn-out of the thigh, which should be held motion-less and well back during the exercise. **D2, 3** and **4** constitute the preparation before music begins which is a moderate waltz tempo. Each 'round' is accompanied by one bar of music, the first beat of which always finds the working leg extended *à la seconde*, the third when it is touching the calf of the supporting leg. Study the plans of all *ronds de jambe* carefully (page 32, **A7** and **A8**; above, **D6**): neither should be a complete circle. Above also : **D4** shows *en dedans*, **D5** *en dehors*.

Développés; battements en cloche

From the verb *développer*, to develop or unfold, *développés* are an exercise to improve control of the legs. This will help in the execution of *adage*, which will be found farther on under Centre Practice. *Développés* are performed to music of slow 3/4 time.

Sequence **A**: **1**, the preliminary position; **2** to **B1**, inclusive, the actual unfolding movement known as a *développé*. They are both done *en croix* here. Take four bars of music for each one. A good method for the beginner, to avoid undue strain, is to do one sequence *en*

A–C

Développés à la barre (en croix): preliminary method

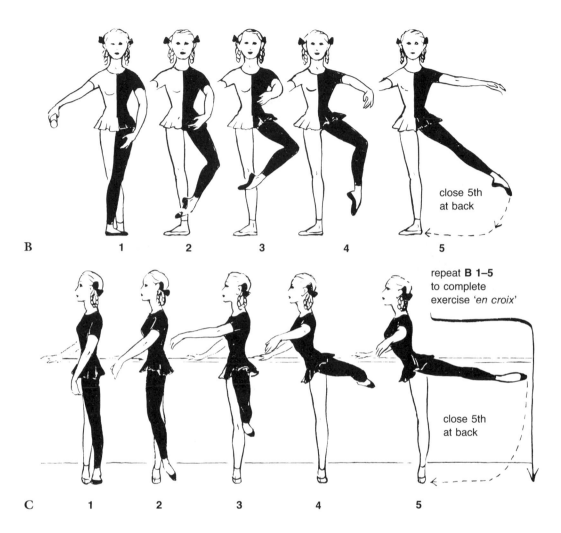

B   1   2   3   4   5

close 5th
at back

repeat **B 1–5**
to complete
exercise '*en croix*'

close 5th
at back

C   1   2   3   4   5

D *développé à la seconde*: example of advanced method

croix with one leg, turn and repeat with the other, and so on. It should be borne in mind that full control of the legs takes many years to accomplish, so do not try to raise the thigh above the level of the hip, as this is in the province of the more advanced student (**D**). A low but well-placed leg is more desirable than one placed very high but turned in, accompanied by contortions of the rest of the body, and too much pressure on the *barre*.

Notice that in sequence **C**, the leg shown in position **4** is passing through *attitude* (see pages 46–7). Note also that only in a *développé* to the back is the body allowed to tilt slightly forward.

Battements en cloche ('like the swing of a bell') are shown in **E**. The purpose of this movement is to produce freedom of the hip socket and to encourage circulation. The preparation is with the working leg *pointe tendue* at the back and the first movement is forward. Take care that both legs are perfectly straight throughout. It is done to a quick 3/4 or slow 6/8 rhythm. If 3/4 time is used, continue swinging the leg back and front until 16 bars have elapsed, or 8 bars of 6/8, using three beats to swing the leg to the front, three to the back.

pass through   1st position

E *battements en cloche*

Relevés from two feet on to one

From the verb *relever*, to rise. *Relevés* are very much used in ballet by both male and female dancers. Here they serve to strengthen the arch of the supporting foot when on *demi-pointe*, which makes it an important exercise for general balance. It also accustoms the dancer to pull up the knee and leg muscles after the comparative relaxation of the *demi-plié*. This stands the dancer in good stead when in actual movement. *Relevés* are also a preparation for *pointe*-work.

Sequence **F**: **b-e**, *relevé devant* (in front); **f-g**, *relevé derrière* (at the back); **h-i**, *relevé passé en arrière* (passed to the back), raising the front foot sharply to the front of the supporting knee, closing 5th at the back; **j-k**, *relevé passé en avant* (passed to the front), raising the back foot quickly to the back, side and front of the supporting knee before closing 5th in front.

The term *relevé* really relates to the **supporting** foot which rises sharply to the *demi-pointe* by means of a slight spring, in the manner shown in the first drawing. After each *relevé*, both feet return to their original positions simultaneously, again with a slight spring.

the supporting foot
in *relevés à la barre*

(right foot)

slight spring

count

Centre practice (exercices au milieu)

Having completed the preceding work at the *barre*, which should take the average student about half an hour, the body should be sufficiently 'warmed up' to start work without the aid of the *barre*. For when the circulation is running properly one can feel and control the muscles with comparative ease.

For the first two months, in order that the student may become thoroughly acquainted with *barre* exercises, the latter of them should be repeated in the centre of the room without the aid of the *barre* (but beginners should except *battements sur le cou de pied, sur la demi-pointe* and *battements en cloche*). When working in the centre the arm which rested on the *barre* should make exactly the same movements as the working arm.

After two months, the student may begin to combine these *barre* exercises in various ways, e.g. 8 counts of *battements frappés* followed by 8 counts of *battements sur le cou de pied* with the same foot, and the same the other side. After this, the *barre* exercises may be used in conjunction with other movements of the arms and body, in the same way that *battements tendus* and *grands battements* are used with the eight directions of the body described on pages 42–3.

As time goes on and the student becomes thoroughly familiar with the *barre* work, some of the repetition in the centre may be omitted, thus leaving more time for practising *adage*, *allegro* and other centre practice.

THE SEVEN MOVEMENTS OF DANCE

There are seven movements of dance which are usually named: *plier* to bend *glisser* to glide *tourner* to turn *étendre* to stretch *sauter* to jump *relever* to raise *élancer* to dart

But because the language of classical dance is French, they are not always used in these forms although the words used may sound similar. The student studying for examinations would do well to study the following chart and examples of how the terms can vary.

		VERB	ADJECTIVE	NOUN
1	to bend	*plier*	—	*plié*
2	to stretch	*étendre*	*tendu* or *tendue*	—
3	to rise	*relever*	*relevé*	*relevé*
4	to jump	*sauter*	*sauté*	*saut*
	ALSO	*jeter*	*jeté*	*jeté*
5	to glide	*glisser*	*glissé*	*glissade*
	ALSO	*chasser*	*chassé*	*chassé*
6	to dart	*élancer*	*élancé*	—
7	to turn	*tourner*	*tourné*	*tour*

Examples

1 two *demi-* and one full *pliés* = two half bends and one full bend
2 two *battements tendus* = two knocks with the leg stretched
3 one *battement relevé* = one knock with the leg raised
  two *relevés sur les pointes* = two rises on pointes
4 *retiré sauté* = a jumped *retiré*
  two *sauts* in 1st = two jumps in 1st position
5 two *battements glissés* = two glided knocks
  glissade devant = *glissade* (glided step) to the front
6 *glissade élancé* = a glided step not along the floor but darted over the surface
7 two *tours en l'air* = two turns in the air
  one *détourné* = a turned closing of the feet

THE FIVE BASIC POSITIONS OF THE ARMS

To show the basic positions of the arms, the Cecchetti system has been adopted. These positions remain more or less the same as taught by other methods, but the order may differ. The student should memorise these positions immediately because, like the five positions of the feet, dancing cannot take place without them.

Attention is drawn to the 1st position in which the little finger of each hand should be about 2 in. (5 cm) away from the sides of the boy's thighs (about 4 in. (10 cm) away for girls). The same applies to 5th position *en bas* (low). The girl should always imagine that her fingers never touch the edge of her tutu.

In all these positions the shoulders should be kept **down**, particularly in 5th *en haut* (high) when it is very easy to hunch them. The elbows should never be allowed to cave in and should always be supported (which will make them ache, but never mind). The wrist should also be supported in all positions and never be allowed to flap either up or down. The fingers are held closely together with the thumb pulled slightly towards the palm of the hand. A soft, clear line should be practised from shoulder to fingertips, controlled but never strained in appearance. All disagreeable angles such as 'broken' wrists, pointed elbows and crooked little fingers should be avoided with very great care.

5th position of the feet

1st

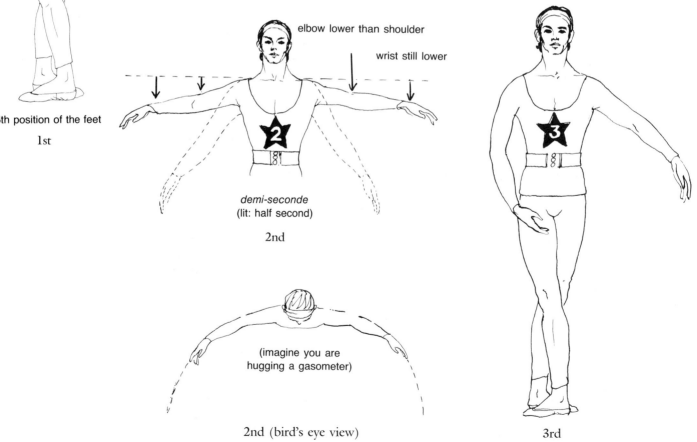

elbow lower than shoulder

wrist still lower

demi-seconde
(lit: half second)

2nd

(imagine you are
hugging a gasometer)

2nd (bird's eye view)

3rd

4th *en haut*

5th *en haut*

5th *en bas*

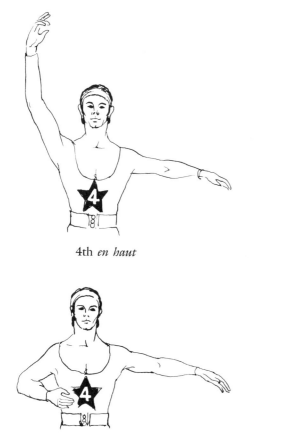

4th *en avant*

5th *en avant*

5th *en avant*
(bird's eye view)

Miscarriage of the arms!

In the days when ballet dancers did not show their legs, the arms received a great deal more attention than they do today. The same thing applied to young people in ordinary life, so that anyone taking 'dancing class' had a head start, having been trained to sit up straight, take their elbows off the table, etc., from early childhood.

Now the legs tend to receive almost undivided attention, which is deeply regrettable. Quite tiny girls can perform thirty-two *fouettés* – but usually fail to attract admiration, or employment, with arms that whack them round and round like two broken propellers. And ballets like *Les Sylphides*, in which the legs are covered, become increasingly hard to watch.

On this spread, the whole figure is drawn in addition to the arm positions to underline the fact that you will never succeed in controlling your arms if you do not stand properly. Although the mirror will help you to work on your arms, watch out also for your facial expression: take away the mirror and the face is apt to register a lost and vacuous look. It is a good idea to practise your arm positions with your eyes closed. Then open them and compare what you thought you were doing with what you really look like.

It is something else again to move from one position to another, but the exercises in *port de bras* which follow are designed to help you.

Although choreographers may ask you to use your arms in many different ways, you will not be able to follow instructions if you cannot control your arms in the first place.

A first exercise in *port de bras*

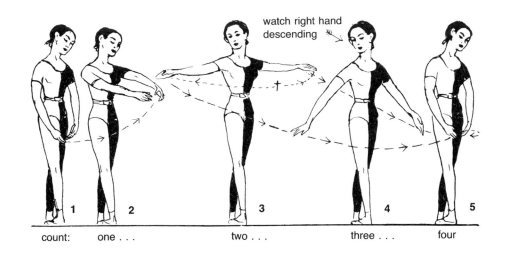

watch right hand descending

count: one . . .   two . . .   three . . .   four

Exercises in port de bras (carriage of the arms)

Generally speaking, the word 'expression' is applied to the face alone; but the exercises in *port de bras* shown here are a first study in the expressive use of the arms. Moreover, the ballet dancer is not confined to the expression of anger, pleasure, fear, etc., but the whole body is constantly called upon to interpret many shades of poetic emotion to accompany the various kinds of music. The arms are the most expressive part of the body, apart from the face, for showing these delicate nuances.

In the four exercises illustrated, the body faces a *croisé* direction (see position termed *croisé devant* on page 42). A slow 3/4 time music should be used; 4 bars should accompany each sequence and each sequence should be performed four times facing the two opposite corners of the room. The arms and head should move together smoothly and continuously, avoiding jerkiness and pauses. Here is the first opportunity of applying in centre practice all you have learned at the *barre* concerning posture: knees must be pulled up, body must be straight and slim; and remember, also, all you have been told about the use of the arms: shoulders down, rounded, supported elbows and simple hands.

Pay careful attention to the illustrations and note whether the head is inclined, turned, raised or lowered.

In relation to the established positions of the arms: in the second exercise (**B**), the arms start in 5th *en bas* (**B1**); right arm brushes through 1st position into an *arabesque* position (see page 45, left arm of **b**); at the same time the left arm passes through 5th *en avant* into a variation of the position known as *attitude* (**B2**). From there, both arms (travelling different ways) pass into 2nd (**B3**), into *arabesque* (**B5**) and to 5th *en bas* again (**B6**) and so on.

These exercises are more difficult than they appear at first glance, as they feature independent control of the arms at the same time, e.g. **B1–2**. Here it is obvious that the left arm has a considerable distance to travel, the right arm only a short distance, but both arms must reach the position shown in **2** simultaneously, neither of them pausing en route. Do not be discouraged if it is difficult at first: dancers take years to perfect their arms. If you look at any action photograph you will see proof of this.

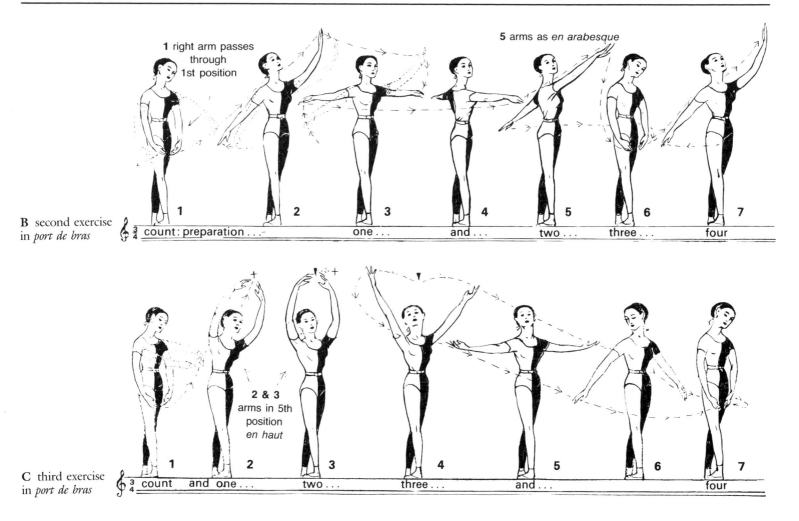

1 right arm passes through 1st position

5 arms as *en arabesque*

B second exercise in *port de bras*

$\frac{3}{4}$ count: preparation ... one ... and ... two ... three ... four

2 & 3 arms in 5th position *en haut*

C third exercise in *port de bras*

$\frac{3}{4}$ count and one ... two ... three ... and ... four

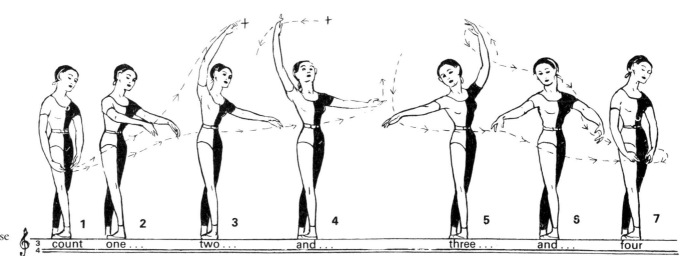

D fourth exercise in *port de bras*

$\frac{3}{4}$ count one ... two ... and ... three ... and ... four

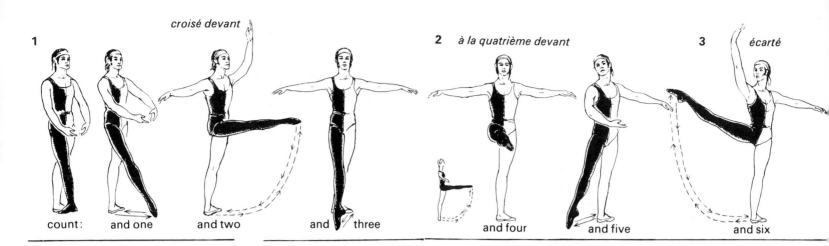

croisé devant — 1

count: and one   and two   and three

2   *à la quatrième devant*   3   *écarté*

and four   and five   and six

4   *effacé*   5   *à la seconde*   6   *épaulé*

and seven   and eight   and nine   and ten   close behind   and eleven   and twelve   and thirteen

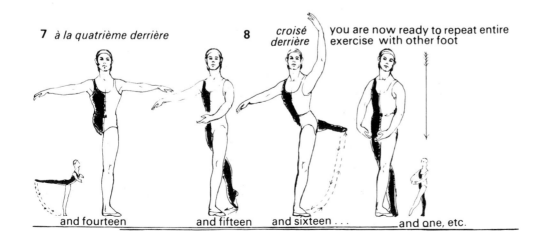

7   *à la quatrième derrière*   8   *croisé derrière*   you are now ready to repeat entire exercise with other foot

and fourteen   and fifteen   and sixteen . . .   and one, etc.

THE EIGHT DIRECTIONS OF THE BODY

The eight directions of the body are as follows:

1 *croisé devant* (crossed front)
2 *à la quatrième devant* (to the fourth front)
3 *écarté* (separated, or thrown wide apart)
4 *effacé* (shaded)
5 *à la seconde* (to the second)
6 *épaulé* (shouldered)
7 *à la quatrième derrière* (to the fourth back)
8 *croisé derrière* (crossed back)

Like the five positions of the feet and arms, the eight directions of the body govern many of the movements in dancing. They should therefore be memorised by the student as quickly as possible.

An exercise with battements tendus and grands battements

The illustrations show the eight directions linked by *battements tendus*, with a *grand battement* performed in each of the main postures. **The legs and body change direction at the same time that the *battement tendu* is being performed**. As in the preceding exercises in *port de bras*, the arms should move smoothly and continuously, avoiding jerkiness.

Pirouettes

From the French verb *pirouetter*, 'to whirl', in ballet a *pirouette* denotes spinning on one leg. Here we have chosen a *pirouette en dehors* and in *demi-pointe* because this is usual for the beginner, but there are many other kinds.

The four sequences **A**, **B**, **C** and **D** show an exercise in *pirouettes en dehors* in quarter turns.

A Stand facing front, feet 5th position with left foot front. With the front or working foot, execute *tendu* to the side, taking the arms to 2nd position. Working foot now traces a *demi rond de jambe en dehors*, ending in 4th *croisé* with a *demi-plié*. At the same time the left arm moves forward to 5th *en avant*. Bring the arms sharply down to 5th *en bas*, *relevé* raising the working foot in front, at the same time making a quarter turn towards raised foot. Then close feet together with a slight spring into *demi-plié*, working foot in front (see *relevés* on page 36), opening the arms slightly forward as shown in illustration. This completes the first quarter turn.

Follow the same instructions for **B**, **C** and **D**, as illustrated; then put the other foot in front and repeat the other way.

A, **B**, **C** and **D** four quarter turns as preliminary exercise for *pirouettes en dehors*

(*Continued overleaf*)

focus on point straight ahead   turn head sharply

E use of head during complete *pirouettes* (here *en dehors*)

After practising the quarter turns and before attempting the complete *pirouette*, **half** turns should be practised with the same head principles applied as in **E**.

Sequence **E** illustrates a single complete *pirouette*. The rules are the same as for the quarter turns except that the use of the head comes into play, in order to prevent giddiness, to gain impetus and to give a brilliant effect. The idea is to focus the eyes on a spot directly in front, to look at it for as long as possible whilst the body is turning, then to bring the head sharply round to the front again before the body has finished turning.

Music should be 4/4 time for all these exercises; the *tendu* is done to the first beat, *demi-plié* in fourth to the second beat, *relevé* to the third beat and closing of the feet to the fourth beat in the bar.

First arabesque

An *arabesque* is a beautiful pose which has now become a household word and hardly needs introduction to the general reader. From the point of view of execution, however, it is not such a simple matter.

The first step towards performing a good *arabesque* is to dispense completely with the idea that the essence of this pose is to stand on one leg and then kick the back one as high as possible. The quality of an *arabesque* will improve only as the quality of your technique improves. A good *arabesque* will be the reward of the student who has worked hard at the rather boring aspects of ballet technique at the *barre*: general posture, which includes well-controlled feet, pulled-up knee muscles and straight body. If the student has not bothered to attend to these important details the result will be ungainly poses. The correct execution of *grands battements* at the back (see page 31) is very important, with the upper part of the body tilted slightly forward, the chest raised, and the supporting leg straight. An *arabesque* is a pose of quality rather than an acrobatic feat – this is why it is in an *arabesque* that the characters of various students show most strongly; whether they are lazy, flashy, conceited or have good taste.

There are many different kinds of *arabesque* but the *first arabesque*, as shown, is the most familiar of all and also the one which is learned first by the beginner. **A** shows a *first*

A(i) *chassé à la quatrième en avant*
A(ii) *first arabesque (à terre)*
A(iii) *first arabesque*

B *first arabesque (allongée)*
C *first arabesque penchée*

arabesque preceded by a *chassé* from a *demi-plié* in the 5th position. (*Chasser*, here 'to slide') In this case: slide the front foot forward until the weight of the body is distributed equally between the legs; straighten both knees, at the same time transferring the weight of the body on to the front leg, stretching the back foot into *pointe tendue* and using the arms as shown in **Aii**. This pose is known as *first arabesque à terre* (on the ground). Slowly raise the back leg a few inches from the ground without moving the body. When you feel you have lifted your leg in this way as high as physically possible, allow the body to tilt slightly forward, raising the back leg at the same time (**Aiii**). After a few months' study you may tilt the body further and attempt an *arabesque allongée* (lengthened) as in **B**.

C shows a *penchée* (pitched) position as the final aspect of the *first arabesque*, but this pose should not be attempted by first-year students.

chassé à la quatrième en avant

attitude croisée à terre
(on the ground)

bird's eye view of leg
correctly raised *en attitude*

body turned towards
downstage left

Attitude croisée

croisée

beginners:
do not try to
raise your
leg higher
than this

effacée

Attitudes, croisée and effacée

The pose known as *attitude* is based on a
famous figure of Mercury by Gian Bologna
(or Jean de Bologne). It has much in
common with the *arabesque*: not only is it a
beautiful pose in itself, but also it is much
used in the course of actual dance movement – jumps and turns are performed *en
attitude* and *en arabesque*, and both figure

chassé à la quatrième en avant

body turned towards downstage right

attitude effacée à terre
(on the ground)

Attitude effacée

largely in the execution of *adage*. One of the most lovely and effective movements in ballet is the turn *en attitude*, but this is for the more advanced student.

Attitude croisée: for a preparation, stand facing a *croisé* direction (see page 42), right foot front. Execute a *chassé* as shown (**2** and **3**) into *attitude à terre*, with the width of the body well over the front foot. Note the inclination of the head towards the raised arm. Raise the back leg *en l'air* by lifting the thigh, into *attitude croisée*, as shown in the illustration. In all basic *attitudes* the knee should be higher from the ground than the foot. (See page 35, **C4**, at the *barre*)

To perform *attitude effacée*, stand in an *effacé* position (see page 42). Follow the drawing, using the same method as for *attitude croisée*.

Adage

chassé à la quatrième en avant · attitude croisée à terre · attitude croisée en l'air

1 2 3 4 5 four

Valse, op. 69, no. 1, Chopin

p con espressione

Notes on adage

Adage is the French version of *ad agio*, an Italian musical term for 'at ease' which usually means 'slow-moving'. In ballet it describes a slow dance in which all parts of the body are used simultaneously to give a harmonious effect. The onlooker may find such an exercise soothing to watch, but it is anything but 'leisurely' for the dancer.

When the teacher says, 'Let us do some *adage*', this means that several steps are to be combined together to make a slow poetic dance. Usually a different combination is given each time, and this gives the student practice at rapidly picking up and memorising sequences of steps, and mastering the various difficulties of execution which usually occur when passing from one step to another. This is another occasion when the character and musical sense of the student begin to take shape and evolve.

Exercises in adage – an example

An example of an elementary *adage* is given here. Taking the movements one by one, they are as follows:

1–3 *chassé*
4 *attitude croisée à terre*
5 *attitude croisée en l'air*
6 *attitude en face*
7 *attitude effacée* INTO
8 *arabesque fondue allongée* with the arms *en*

attitude (*fondue* from *fondre*, 'to sink', signifying a bend on one leg with the other raised)
9–12 *pas de bourrée dessus* (see page 53, **C**)
13–15 *développé* into *second arabesque* (*second arabesque* is the same as *first* but with the other leg raised); and so through **16–20** INTO
21 *arabesque fondue allongée*
22–24 *pas de bourrée dessous* into 4th position of the feet
25–28 *pirouette en dehors*

When a pivot is made on one leg (as in **5**, **6** and **7** and later in **16–20**) the movement is termed a *promenade*.

The music chosen for this *adage* is Chopin's *Valse*, op. 69, which has been arranged here so that the bars coincide with the dancer's movements in order to give the idea of accompaniment. Note also that the music is headed *con espressione*, 'with expression', which is the kind of music you should always choose for *adage*. Some of Chopin's *Nocturnes* are also suitable.

Until this point, the music accompanying the exercises has been indicated merely as 6/8, 4/4, etc., because its main purpose has been to provide a rhythmic accompaniment for the steps. Arranging an *adage* to music, however, is a far more subtle matter. A technical knowledge of music, as well as a natural musical sense, is of the greatest possible value to ballet teachers, students and critics.

attitude en face   attitude effacée

pas de bourrée dessous

movements   of heel

into second arabesque

developpé   cou de pied   five movements

of heel

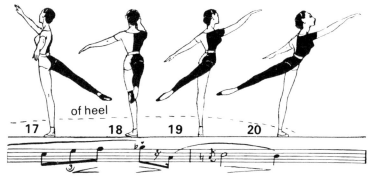

arabesque fondue allongée

pirouette en dehors

repeat exercise on other side

Allegro and steps of elevation

General observations

Musically, the term *allegro* indicates 'quick and lively'. In ballet the term embraces many steps, among them the gliding movements called *glissades*, the brilliant, intricate *pas de bourrée*, the little jumps called *sautés* and the long smooth leaps known as *grands jetés*. Sometimes there is a distinction between steps of the same name when performed in different ways, e.g. *échappés sautés* (page 54) which are a large movement compared with the pizzicato effect of *échappés relevés sur les pointes* (page 61).

Steps of *allegro* are NEVER attempted till the body is perfectly 'warmed up'. Many accidents are due to failure to note this classic regulation.

In the course of the graceful *arabesques* and *attitudes* and the slow elegance of *adage*, a certain type of dancer shows to advantage – the loose-limbed, supple individual with high insteps. With the introduction of *pas d'allegro*, however, the opposite type scores – the stockier, broader person who usually has strong, flat feet and clearly defined muscles. Briefly, the first type tends towards a knock-knee and usually has an inborn facility for slow, graceful movement; the second has a tendency towards bandiness and at the same time a natural dexterity in sharp, brilliant movement, an excellent sense of timing and good elevation. Both these physical defects can be greatly minimised (in many cases, cured) by exercises at the *barre* and care in basic deportment. Each type should work particularly hard at those steps which are the hardest for him or her to master.

A well-known dancer of the second, less graceful type, was described thus by a spectator: 'You only notice his face when he is doing slow movements, and he must be quite heavy; but when he moves fast – whew! he flashes about like a shrimp in a puddle!'

In steps of *allegro* it is very important to pay heed to neatness, vitality of expression, and control of the arms.* Also, do not make the mistake of thinking that because the steps are small they are insignificant, for small steps should flash like quicksilver.

Strongly made types often experience initial difficulty with the small, neat but important steps. Often, however, they are gifted with a remarkable power of elevation and leap much higher than their classmates. Now it is more usual to see a beginner jumping too high than a finished performer, but the uncontrolled leaper will lose his power of elevation, due to physical injuries – unless he is willing to study the science of leaping in ballet.

Although a great elevation can be a tremendous asset, it can also be dangerous in its early stages. Jumping in ballet is not a sport, and height is by no means the sole object. Positioning in the air and a graceful landing are equally important.

To describe how to control and increase elevation would be a lengthy subject. Here, therefore, I shall give only the main essentials governing the first steps of elevation in ballet. They should be carefully studied.

1 A good preparation ensures a good jump. Whether the spring comes from both feet, as in *échappés sautés changés* on page 54 or from one foot, as shown in *jetés derrière* on page 55, a good 'bend' of the knees with the heels firmly on the ground is essential. (Try a jump without bending the knees and see what happens!) Without bending the knees, the heels – which are responsible for

---

* A small movement looks ridiculous if accompanied by flapping arms.

all elevation – cannot give you a good push upwards.

2 Once in the air, it is essential that the knees and feet are as straight, i.e. as fully stretched, as possible – not only for appearances' sake, but to ensure a soft, correct **and safe** landing.

3 Taking the landing from a jump in slow motion: the toes should be the first to touch the ground, and passing rapidly through the intermediate foot positions (see page 27, **3c**, **b** and **a**) the heels should follow, the movement being completed with a *demi-plié* of the knees.

A jump which is not followed by a *demi-plié* is liable to break your knees for you – no less. If you do bend your knees on landing, but insufficiently, you will make a noise like a house falling down.

Failure to bring the heels down to the ground after each step of elevation tends to thicken the Achilles tendon. As this is a common fault amongst ballet dancers, it has given rise to the popular belief that the study of ballet leads to thick ankles. **Improperly performed**, it does.

Sauté, changement and glissades
(as shown on pages 51 and 52)

1 *Sauté* is from *sauter*, 'to jump'. It is advisable to execute sixteen of these little jumps continuously to warm and strengthen the feet as a prelude to steps of *allegro*. They are performed in the 1st position of the feet.

2 *Changement* is from *changer*, 'to change', so called because the feet change position in mid-air, **on the way down** each time. Perform sixteen. In these two exercises do not tilt the body either backwards or forwards.

3 *Glissade* is from *glisser*, 'to glide'. When following the illustrations be careful not to give a jerky effect: the five figures in each sequence are part of one complete movement. At first the *glissades* should be practised slowly and smoothly to a 3/4 time, with the last figure of each sequence coinciding with the first beat of the bar. Gradually increase the speed until

1 *sauté*

2 *changement*

3(i) *glissade derrière*

3(ii) *glissade devant*

3(iii) *glissade dessus*

3(iv) *glissade dessous*

3(v) *glissade en avant*

slide forwards

3(vi) *glissade en arrière*

slide backwards

4 three *glissades* (*derrière*) with *changements* as an exercise (note use of arms)

the movement becomes sharp and neat. Carefully memorise the different placing of the feet and the special head movement which goes with each.

4 An example of *glissades* as they may be used one after another to make a little exercise.

Note   *derrière* behind   *devant* in front *dessus* over   *dessous* under   *en avant* coming forward   *en arrière* going backwards.

When using these terms to describe an *assemblé* it is useful to remember that the *assemblé* can either be *en place* without moving from the spot it began, or *porté* travelling.

Pas de bourrée

Musically speaking, a *bourrée* denotes a dance in 2/4 time starting with an up-beat. In ballet there are countless varieties of *bourrée*. They are not only used as steps by themselves but are also used to move from one position to another: when a dancer crosses the stage with tiny twinkling steps *sur les pointes*, this is a species of *bourrée*. The examples below are the first ones you will learn in class.

Study the illustrations carefully. Note that in **E** and **F*** the body on both occasions faces an *effacée* direction. *Pas de bourrée en avant* and *en arrière* are often performed together as an exercise going forwards and backwards, so the last drawing in each sequence shows the figure ready to move in the opposite direction. For a single example of each of these two steps, close the foot in 5th position, as in the previous *pas de bourrée* (**A** to **D**).

* see page 54

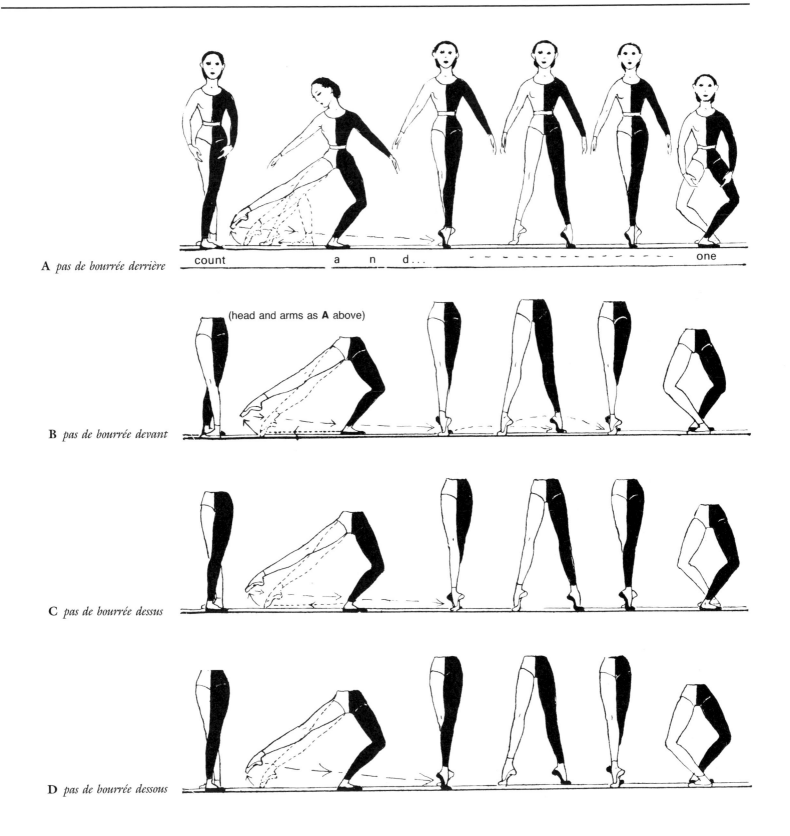

A *pas de bourrée derrière*

count   a   n   d...   one

(head and arms as **A** above)

B *pas de bourrée devant*

C *pas de bourrée dessus*

D *pas de bourrée dessous*

E *pas de bourrée en avant*

(*effacé* direction)

F *pas de bourrée en arrière*

Echappes sautés changés

Echappé is from *échapper*, 'to escape'

Perform the sequence four times (**2–10**), jumping as high as possible with a big *demi-plié*. Get your breath; then repeat in a smaller, quicker manner.

Jetés derrière and devant

Jeté is from *jeter*, 'to throw'

There are many different kinds of *jeté*, but the examples shown to the right are the first that you will learn in class. This is the first time that you spring from one leg to land on the other. You must not travel sideways: *jetés derrière* – travel forward the width of one of your feet with each step; *jetés devant* – backwards. It is best to try them in a small way at first: eight *derrière* and eight *devant* with alternate feet. Repeat the exercise more slowly and with higher elevation as you progress. The working foot brushes the ground and this pushes you upwards. Make sure that for a second both the legs are straight in the air.

Echappés sautés changés

1	2	3	4	5	6
count		and	one	and	two, etc.

7   8   9   10

Jeté derrière   *Jeté devant*

Jetés derrière with *temps levés*

count   and   one   and   two

and   three   and   four

A *assemblé derrière*

1   2   3   slide left foot   4   5

B *assemblé devant*

1   2   3   4   5

Jetés derrière

Here the *jetés* are arranged as an exercise with *temps levés* ('lifted' steps, or hops).

Assemblés; soubresauts

Assemblé from *assembler*, 'to put together'; *soubresaut*, 'a jump' – a straight jump with the feet in 5th position

The feet are put together in the air, before landing. In the sequences **A** and **B**, stage **4** is where the most common mistake occurs. You **must** assemble your feet before landing. Again, as in *jetés*, you gain impetus for your jump by brushing the working foot along the ground before taking off. It takes quite a while to learn this movement, but once learned, it will be possible to try the little exercise shown in **E**, composed of *glissades*, *assemblés* and a *soubresaut*. Pay special attention to the use of the head – there are a few catches.

C *assemblé dessus*

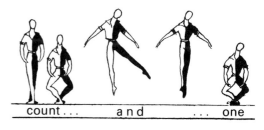

count . . .   a n d   . . . one

D *assemblé dessous*

E exercise with *glissades*, *assemblés* and *soubresaut*

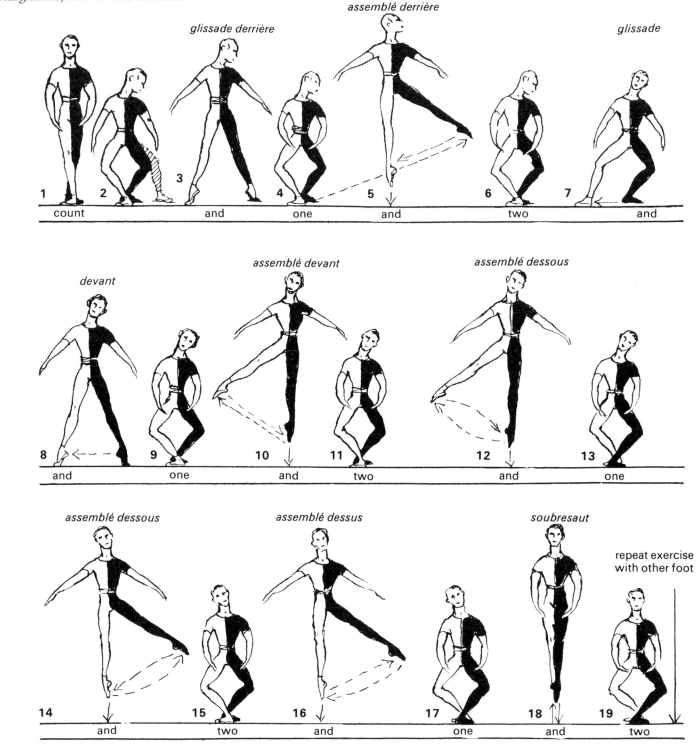

glissade derrière   assemblé derrière   glissade

1	2	3	4	5	6	7
count		and	one	and	two	and

devant   assemblé devant   assemblé dessous

8	9	10	11	12	13
and	one	and	two	and	one

assemblé dessous   assemblé dessus   soubresaut

repeat exercise with other foot

14	15	16	17	18	19
and	two	and	one	and	two

Grands jetés, en avant and en tournant ('turning')

Pas de bourrée courus (preparatory running steps) and *grand jeté en avant*

slide foot through

The illustrations show two sorts of *grands jetés* practised by a girl familiar with the movements. Some beginners, however, find it difficult to master the basic 'mechanics' of these beautiful and effective leaps. The best way of learning to perform them is to follow the illustrations closely – but hardly to leave the ground at first in the leap itself. Elevation can be increased directly the student has mastered the actual method. The drawings also show the 'preparatory runs' for both types of *jeté*, from which the dancer should gain impetus for both the height and the length of the leap.

Grand jeté en tournant

slide

nos
cover dista
equal to two pa

to continue exercise
repeat movement
as from no. 3

en into leap

to continue exercise:
repeat movement
as from no. 2

careful how you land

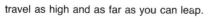

nos 7–10:
travel as high and as far as you can leap.

Sur les pointes

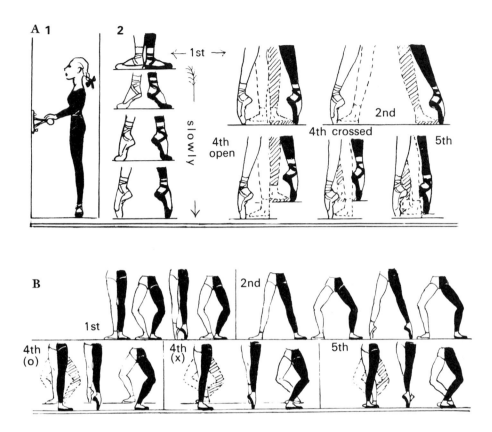

Preliminary notes

The girls shown in the illustrations on these two pages are all over ten years of age and have been regularly studying for two years the other exercises described in this book. They therefore have a right to be on their *pointes*. Even so, **all these exercises are performed with aid of the *barre*.**

Some girls rise on their *pointes* easily and naturally and others need to fit and adjust their shoes very carefully. As the foot or feet rise through quarter, half, three-quarter to full *pointe* the weight must be centred correctly through the bones of the leg and foot. Ideally a dancer stands on three toes. But few feet are so made, thus ankles, insteps and toes must be strengthened before any attempt is made at *pointe*-work. The first pair of *pointe* shoes should always be fitted by an expert. In general the shoe must never allow for growing but must fit snugly.

and   one   and   two   and   one   and   two   (etc.)

D *échappés en croix*

First exercises

A1 The correct stance for exercises facing the *barre*, i.e. **A–D** inclusive.

    Beginners should not hesitate to place a lot of weight on the *barre* at first, to protect the feet from strain until they grow stronger.

A2 For slow *relevés* the knees should be perfectly straight throughout.

    The same *relevés* should then be performed to brisk tempo, several in each position.

B *Relevés* should then be repeated in basic positions with *demi-pliés*.

C The *relevés* on half-*pointe* (from two feet to one foot) shown on page 36 may be performed now on full *pointe*.

D This exercise in *échappés en croix*, shown here on full *pointe*, should be included after the *relevés* on full *pointe*, among the more advanced *barre* exercises.

E *Posés* mean 'steady!' The movement with the white leg (**2–4**) should be as quick as possible. Practise these *posés* slowly and carefully at first, gradually increasing speed.

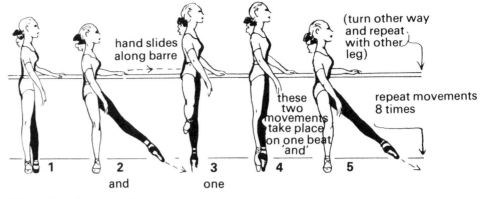

E1 *posé coupé en avant à terre*

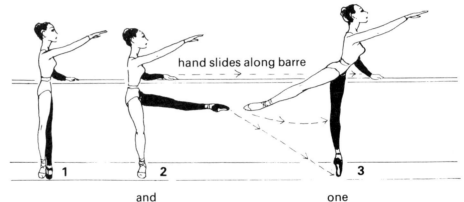

E2 *posé coupé en l'air*
posés coupés with *développés*

STAGE COSTUME

Classical female dress

Use flame-proof fabrics whenever possible

Wearing a tutu marks the final stage in a female dancer's training, for nothing reveals so clearly the perfection of Classical technique as the brief, full skirt and tightly fitting sleeveless bodice. Similarly, the longer Romantic ballet skirt shows a dancer's ability to create from the cold academic formulae of the classroom a flowing pattern of lyrical movement. By kind permission of Dame Ninette de Valois we reproduce here the two patterns for tutu and longer ballet skirt made by the late Miss Olivia Cranmer of the Royal Opera House, Covent Garden. All those who have seen the Royal Ballet and companies of its

stature will realise the importance of these costumes. They should also realise the infinite care and patience with which each detail has been designed and perfected.

THE TUTU

A tutu should be earned by hard work – nothing looks more ludicrous than untrained legs and bodies under this highly professional skirt which reveals every leg movement. Tutus should be used for practice as well as performance so that you get accustomed to

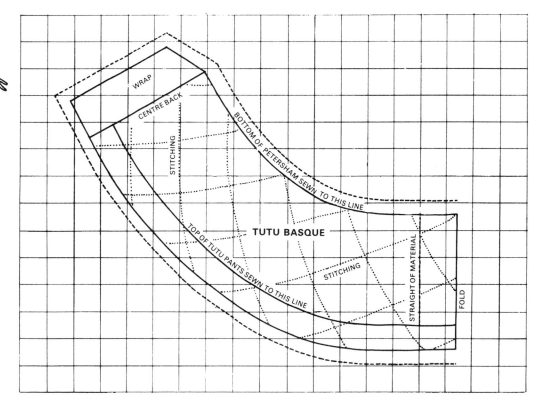

Pattern of tutu basque (see note about size of grid squares on page 15)

the fact that you cannot see the feet and that a tight bodice needs a well-controlled body. Moreover the arms have to be held very carefully so that they at no time spoil the line of the skirt.

It should be noted that for double-work (dance with a partner) it is not advisable to apply any form of decoration between bust and hip. Any decoration embracing the whole dress, or covering the waistline and basque (such as swan's wings with an Odette dress in *Swan Lake*) should be added when the tutu is complete.

Decorations added to bodice only, or skirt only, should be completed before bodice and skirt are joined.

Sequins and other decorations to top layer of skirt should be added before it is gathered.

Materials required

Approximately 9 yd (8.25m) of 54 in. (140cm) nylon net or 13 yd (11.75m) of 36 in. (90cm) tarlatan or nylon net; narrow petersham for waist-belt; narrow elastic for knicker legs; 14½ in. (37cm) of elastic 1–1¼ in. (3cm) wide to be stitched through legs; ½ yd (45cm) material for bodice; ¾ yd (70cm) firm cotton fabric for backing bodice; flat hooks and eyes; shoulder straps of ribbon or material; small piece of elastic for shoulder straps.

Waist-belt of narrow petersham, ½–¾ in. (1–2cm) wide is made to fit tightly round waist. Large flat hook and eye are sewn on petersham wrong way round so that they lie flat on dancer's back and do not stick into her spine.

Basque is made of three or four layers of net. These are machined together (see dotted lines on pattern, page 62) to give stability. Centre of basque must be placed on centre fold of material when cutting.

Knickers, made of two layers of net. Cut two pieces. It is essential that the straight of

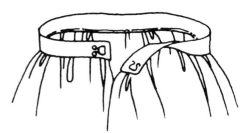

Petersham waist-belt

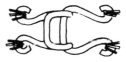

Large hook and eye sewn wrong way round

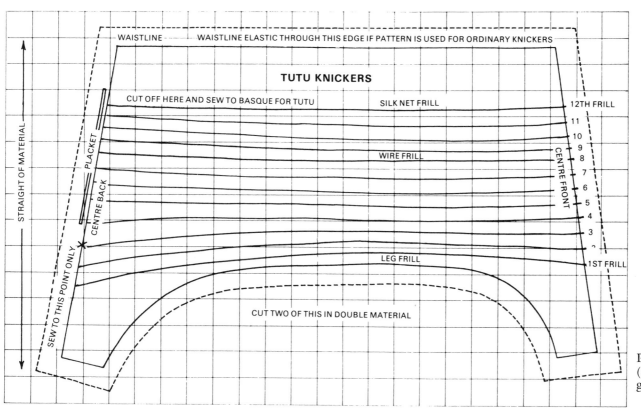

Pattern of tutu knickers (see note about size of grid squares on page 15)

No. of frill	Width of frill (in.)	Width of frill (cm)	Widths of material required 54 in. (140cm)	36 in. (90cm)
Silk net top	12¾	32.5	4	6
12	12½	32	4	6
11	12	30.5	4	6
10	10½	27	4	6
9	9½	24	3½	5
8 (wire frill)	8½	21.5	3½	5
7	7	18	3	4½
6	6	15.5	3	4½
5	5	13	2½	4
4	4	10	2½	4
3	3	7.5	2	3
2	2	5	2	3
1	1½	4	1½	2
Leg frill	1¼	3	1	width for each leg
4	3	3	3	3

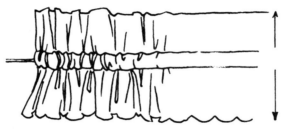

Showing 2 in. (5cm) strip of net and wire, along 8th frill which here has scalloped edge

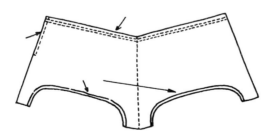

A preparing knickers

B frill sewn on wrong way up

the material is at side of knickers, and that this is sewn at side of basque when joining knicker to basque.

Tutu skirt consists of 12 frills and 1 leg frill, and if required a top frill of silk net. These are cut as shown on the table (left).

The 8th frill usually has a strip of net 2 in. (5cm) wide sewn the length of it, halfway across. This allows for a hoop of crinoline wire to be inserted. This is a light steel band approximately ¾–⅜ in. (1–2cm) wide. Size of hoop varies from 56 to 58 in. (142–147cm) long. The ends of the wire that make the hoop must be properly bound and 4 in. (10cm) extra wire allowed so that there is a proper overlap and that the hoop will not sag (**C**).

The frills must be pinked before gathering. Traditionally Odette-Odile's frills (*Swan Lake*) have outer edges cut in points, while Aurora's (*The Sleeping Beauty*) are cut in scallops. Either edging can be used for other tutus.

Method – skirt

1 Prepare petersham waist-belt and basque, which must be fitted to dancer's figure. Stitch basque to lower edge of petersham.

2 Sew centre front seam of knickers and leave flat.

3 Stitch piece of bias binding round each leg and machine two rows of stitching round top of knickers (**A**).

4 Gather and stitch leg frill round legs, taking care to stitch frill on so that gathered edge faces lower edge of knicker (**B**).

5 Continue gathering and sewing on frills facing wrong way up working from no. 1 to no. 12. Frills are attached ½ in. (1 cm) apart. It is essential that the gathers are absolutely evenly spaced out. Therefore knickers and each frill should be marked out into 8 sections before stitching (**C**).

6 Having stitched on all frills to knickers, stitch up back seam of knickers as far as placket opening. Prepare usual placket opening.

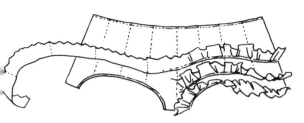

C spacing layers

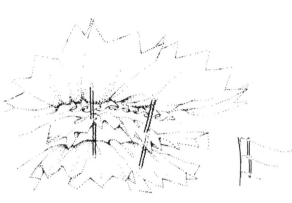

D catch skirts together

E elastic between legs

9 Thread hoop through 8th frill and secure firmly. Sew on small flat hooks and eyes, as on petersham.

10 Frills are now caught together with long stitches (about 3–3½ in. (8cm) long) at 8 in. (20cm) intervals. These stitches are usually made both upwards and downwards from the 8th or 'wire' layer and must be inside skirt, away from the outer edge (**D**).

11 Take a piece of elastic 1–1¼ in. (3cm) wide and 14½ in. (37cm) long and stitch one end firmly to lower edge of basque centre front and the other end to lower edge of basque centre back on same side as the eyes have been sewn (**E**).

Method – bodice

1 Cut out bodice in calico or strong cotton, pin, tack and fit on dancer making sure that side seam is directly centred under the arm, back seam falls straight down spine and front seams fall directly over bust. Mark fitted bodice with tailor's tacks, place cotton backing on bodice material, pin and mark out. Tack backing and bodice material together, then cut out.

2 Stitch bodice seams together, matching marks as indicated and stitching through four thicknesses of material at each seam. Calico or strong cotton backs the bodice material and keeps it firm. Do not line bodice.

3 Stitch bias binding on outside bodice top and lower edge, turn, press and hem on inside. Turn in hem allowance at centre back.

4 Sew on flat hooks and eyes as on petersham.

5 *Boning a bodice* is optional and according to individual requirements. Bones should be covered and well padded at each end. They are sewn in separately and should be placed on top of seams. They can be used under bust, at side seams, at front of bodice and at centre back. (See drawing overleaf.)

Some ballerinas use no boning at all, but have velvet ribbon sewn as indicated in the illustration to prevent bodice slipping.

7 Stitch knicker legs together at crutch and run narrow elastic through hem of legs.

8 Stitch skirt to basque, gathering top of knickers a little and allowing most gathers to fall towards the back of skirt.

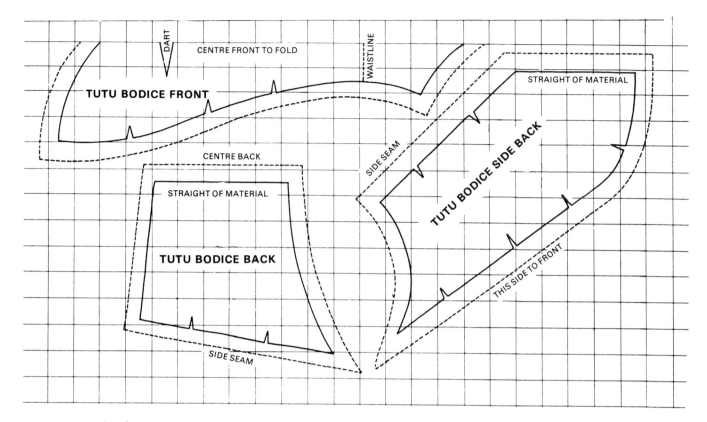

Bodice pattern and how it is placed on material (see note about size of grid squares on page 15). Bodice must be cut very carefully so that straight of material comes exactly as marked on diagram

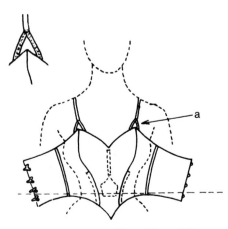

Shoulder straps and position of bones; velvet ribbon can be used instead of bones

Joining bodice to skirt

Bodice should be sewn to lower edge of petersham from centre back to side only. Front of bodice will then fall properly over the basque and it may be caught in one or two places to the basque. However, this catching **must** be done when the dancer is wearing the finished costume.

Shoulder straps, too, must be fitted to suit the dancer. The front ends are attached to top of bodice front seams, the back ends to some point between back and side seams – wherever the dancer finds it most comfortable.

Some dancers like a small piece of elastic added to the front ends of shoulder strap (a). This allows for rise and fall of torso from waist upwards, a movement which is so marked in some dancers. It also prevents the bodice from slipping down or out of place.

THE LES SYLPHIDES AND THE SHORTER SWAN LAKE DRESSES

Both these dresses are made to an identical pattern, the only difference being the length of the skirt (**A**) and the cutting of their edges.

For a *demi-caractère* dress, such as worn by Swanilda in *Coppélia*, use the same patterns for waist-belt, basque, skirt, knickers and bodice as for *Les Sylphides* or *Swan Lake*, shortening the length of skirt to suit the particular dancer.

Les Sylphides skirt is 11 in. (28cm) from the floor, the edge cut in scallops.

Swan Lake skirt is 13 in. (33cm) from the floor, the edge cut in points.

A *demi-caractère* skirt is usually 15 in. (38cm) from the floor, or just below the dancer's knees.

Materials required for skirt, knickers, sleeves and wings

The best material for both *Les Sylphides* and *Swan Lake* skirts is nylon net, but a soft net top skirt is used to advantage on each. **Never** use nylon net for either top skirt as it does not fall softly when the dancer is in movement. It tends to fold into hard lines, particularly in *pirouettes*, and spoils the pattern of the dance.

Each skirt requires layers cut as follows:
Underskirt four widths of 54 in. (140cm) or six widths of 36 in. (90cm) material
2nd skirt four widths of 54 in. or six widths of 36 in. material
Top skirt four widths of 54 in. or six widths of 36 in. material
The depth of each skirt depends upon the height of the dancer. If top skirt measures 31 in. (79cm) in depth from waist to 11 in. (28cm) from floor for a *Sylphides* skirt, then second skirt will be 29½ in. (75cm) deep and underskirt 28 in. (71cm) deep.

The skirts would thus require about 10 yd (9.2m) of 54 in. (140cm) material, plus sufficient tarlatan or nylon net to make basque, a pair of frilled knickers and wing-like sleeves.

Swan Lake

Skirt: method

As in the tutu, the bottom edges of the skirts must be prepared before sewing. In order that the gathers of each skirt be evenly spaced round the basque, both skirts and basque should be marked in equal divisions before the skirts are gathered and attached.

The skirts are sewn on to a basque and waist-belt cut and made up as shown on pages 62–5. The basque is however only 3½ in. (9cm) deep and it is usual to cut this to the tutu pant line shown on page 62. The underskirt is sewn on to the basque 3 in. (8cm) below bottom of petersham waist-belt.

The second skirt is put on 1½ in. (4cm) above this.

Top skirt is stitched to bottom of petersham. (See **B**)

If more skirts are required then the space between the layers should be graduated accordingly.

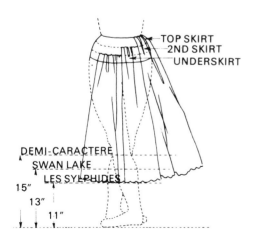

A Lengths of skirt and position of the three layers on the basque

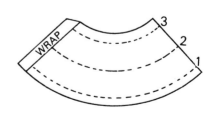

B Where skirts must be sewn to the basque

Knickers: method

Knickers are worn separately with long skirts which are made on a shorter basque.

Cut them to full dimensions of pattern on page 63. Stitch up according to instructions for tutu knickers, using as many frills as felt necessary and spacing these out evenly between the marks for the 1st and 12th frills. Stitch back seam together from lower to upper edges and run elastic through waist-line.

Bodice: materials and method

Amounts of material are the same as for the tutu bodice; dull satin is usually used for *Les Sylphides* and *Swan Lake*. The bodice is made and sewn onto the basque in exactly the same way as for the tutu (see pages 65–6).

Sylphides sleeve

Sylphides wings

Sleeves and wings for Les Sylphides: method

The wing-like sleeves of nylon or soft net are stitched on to the shoulder straps of the bodice. They are sometimes edged with ribbon ¾ in. (2cm) wide.

The wings should be lightly wired and fixed to centre back of waist-line.

Les Sylphides

Classical male dress

THE MALE SHIRT

Pattern – see overleaf.

The male dancer's shirt has many shapes, including the simply-cut magyar sweat shirt. The shirt illustrated is that used by the Royal Danish Ballet in *Napoli*, when it is worn with soft ribbon bow tied and caught at level of top buttonhole. It serves as the basis for the shirt worn in the classroom and also many other ballets. For example: the addition of a deeper collar with pointed ends, and fuller sleeves, turns it into Harlequin's shirt or the male shirt of *Les Sylphides*; with the addition of a yoke cut slightly wider in front so that the collar buttons right up to the neck, it serves with tie, cravat or lace jabot for more formal wear. We are grateful to Neils Bjorn Larsen of the Danish Royal Theatre for permission to use this pattern.

The male shirt

Materials required
$3\frac{1}{4}$–$3\frac{1}{2}$ yd (3m) soft linen, lawn, cotton

Method

1 Having measured and cut shirt, seam back and front together at sides. Use run and fell seams. Turn in hem allowance on fronts.

2 Run two rows of gathering along top of back and along both fronts.

3 Set gathers on to underside of yoke, taking care to fit yoke carefully on shoulder so that shoulder line lies directly on top of shoulder. Set back gathers first.

4 Turn in hem allowance on upper side of yoke, set and machine this over underside of yoke.

5 Seam sleeves together, taking care to fit extra piece exactly as marked in pattern. Use run and fell seams. Turn in hem allowance below mark where seam ends.

6 Set sleeves into armhole, taking care to match underarm seam to side seam. In the normal shirt it should not be necessary to gather top of sleeve. Run and fell seams are usually used.

7 Fold collar in half and seam ends. Turn right side out and set collar on to yoke. Centre back of collar meets centre back of yoke. Edge of collar front meets edge of yoke front.

8 Fold cuff in half, seam ends and turn right side out. Gather lower edge of sleeve and set into cuff, taking care that place for buttonhole falls to outside.

9 Make two buttonholes as indicated on left front, and one buttonhole on outside of each cuff. Sew on buttons to fit buttonholes.

10 Turn in hem allowance round lower edge.

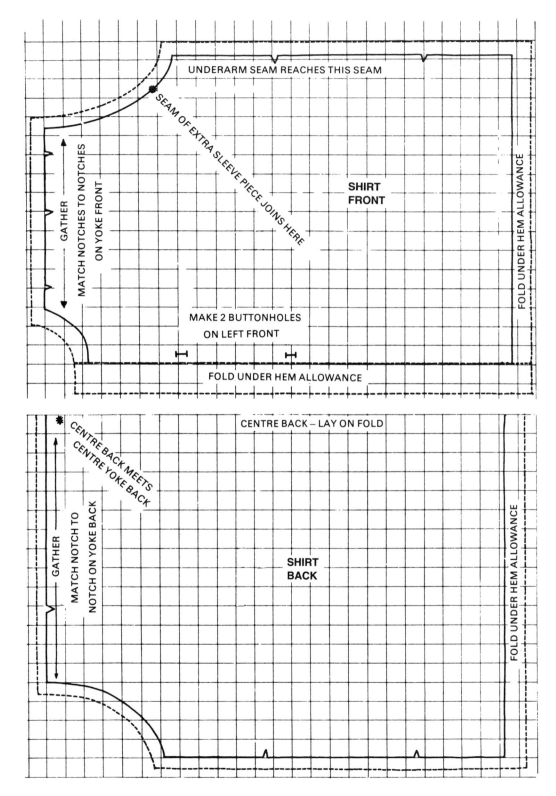

UNDERARM SEAM REACHES THIS SEAM

SEAM OF EXTRA SLEEVE PIECE JOINS HERE

SHIRT FRONT

MATCH NOTCHES TO NOTCHES ON YOKE FRONT

GATHER

FOLD UNDER HEM ALLOWANCE

MAKE 2 BUTTONHOLES ON LEFT FRONT

FOLD UNDER HEM ALLOWANCE

CENTRE BACK – LAY ON FOLD

CENTRE BACK MEETS CENTRE YOKE BACK

MATCH NOTCH TO NOTCH ON YOKE BACK

GATHER

SHIRT BACK

FOLD UNDER HEM ALLOWANCE

Pattern for male shirt: front and back (see note about size of grid squares on page 15)

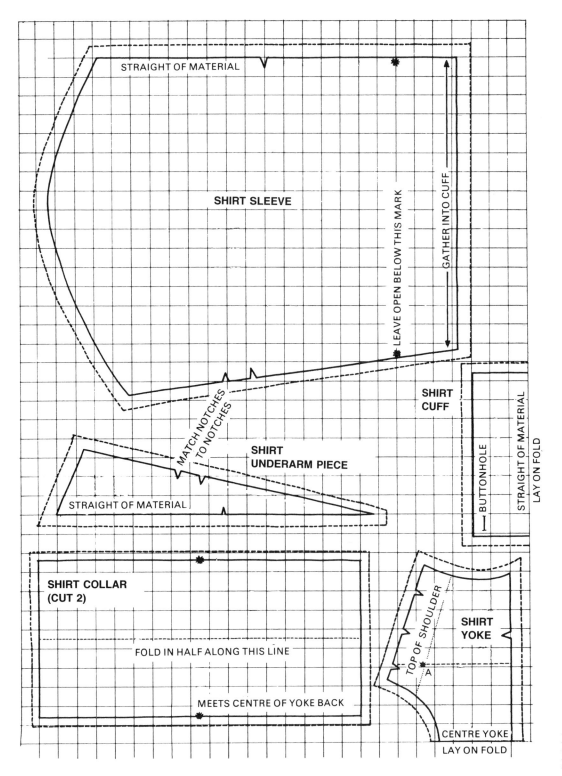

STRAIGHT OF MATERIAL

SHIRT SLEEVE

LEAVE OPEN BELOW THIS MARK

GATHER INTO CUFF

MATCH NOTCHES TO NOTCHES

SHIRT UNDERARM PIECE

STRAIGHT OF MATERIAL

SHIRT CUFF

BUTTONHOLE

STRAIGHT OF MATERIAL

LAY ON FOLD

SHIRT COLLAR (CUT 2)

FOLD IN HALF ALONG THIS LINE

MEETS CENTRE OF YOKE BACK

TOP OF SHOULDER

A

SHIRT YOKE

CENTRE YOKE

LAY ON FOLD

Pattern for male shirt: sleeve and other pieces. Yoke must measure width from shoulder to shoulder

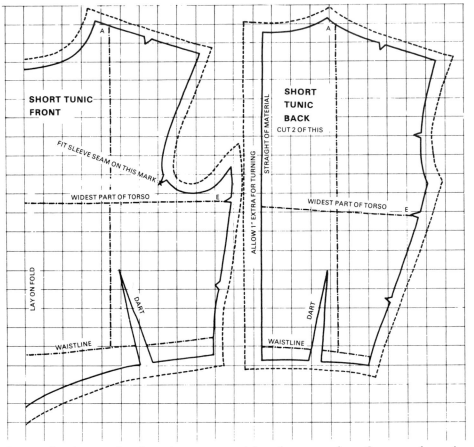

Pattern for short tunic: place pieces on material as shown on chart. See note about size of grid squares on page 15.

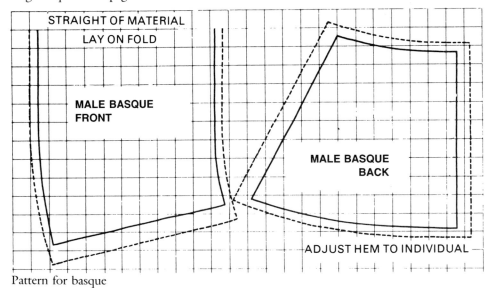

Pattern for basque

MALE TUNICS

The male dancer has great need of a properly-fitting garment if he is to partner the female adequately.

Male tunics for ballet are perhaps the most difficult garments to fit, because the dancer requires much freedom of movement in the torso, particularly if he has lifts to perform. Moreover, it is essential that neither tunic nor sleeve ride up. For this reason it is often wise to set the sleeves on a firm calico or cotton vest. This is cut to the same pattern as the tunic, but reaches only to the waist. The sleeve is then cut a little wider and higher at the top than indicated in the pattern and is set as high as possible **over** the armhole of the vest. The tunic is then cut normally and worn sleeveless, or an épaulette can be added.

The short and long tunics shown here can be easily adapted to a variety of designs.

When cutting the short tunic at least 1 in. (2.5cm) must be added below normal waist-line and lower edge of sleeve to allow for movement. Front darts slope slightly towards the side seams and not straight down the front as in the long tunic. Front of short tunic is wider than front of long tunic because side seams fall to back of armhole, therefore always cut short tunic armholes more deeply in front.

If a longer pointed front is required to short tunic, the whole lower edge from waist must be firmly faced with cotton fabric in addition to calico backing as it is essential that the point remains firm.

If a basque or kilted piece is required, this should be stitched on to short tunic ½ in. (1cm) below normal waistline. Kilted piece is merely a straight piece of material, not too fully pleated, which is stitched to the lower edge of tunic.

Three sleeves are given here. The full sleeve is interchangeable between short and long tunic, but the others are not because the armholes vary in cut. Note very carefully the cut of the straight sleeve in one piece as this is

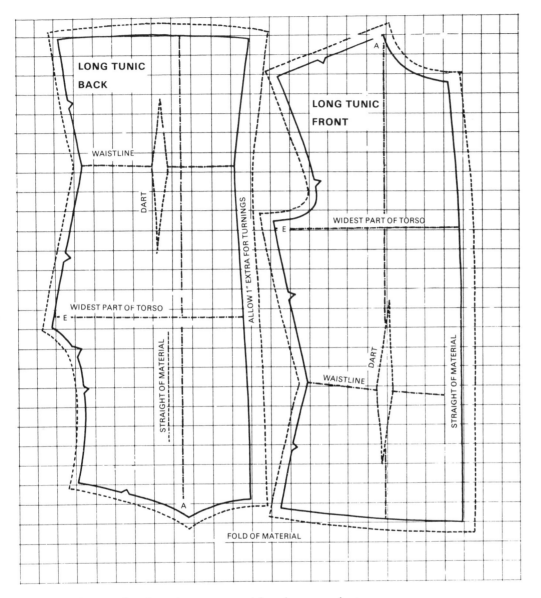

Pattern for long tunic: place pieces on material as shown on chart

Short tunic

Short tunic with basque and épaulettes

designed to give the maximum amount of movement and must on no account be pared down at the top.

The full sleeve and tunic can be properly slashed and the former set over either of the two tighter sleeves. But the slashing can be simulated if you cut pieces of contrasting material slightly larger than shapes indicated in pattern. Pad these pieces slightly and machine them to cut-out material before seaming sleeves. This method is often better, for slashed sleeves and tunic can catch on the girl's dress or hands in double-work.

Male tunics are usually fastened at the back, particularly if double-work is to be performed.

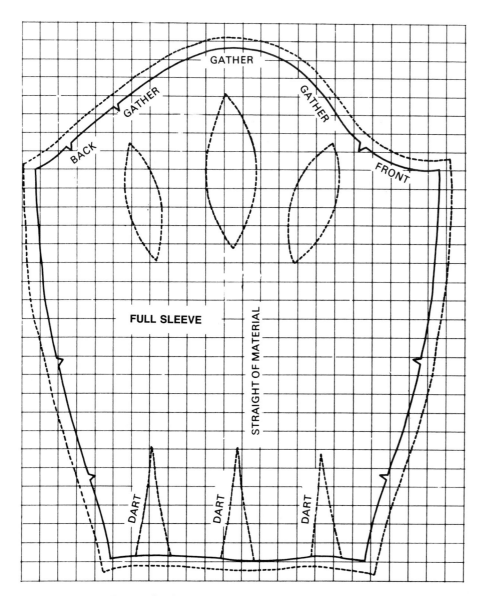

Pattern for full sleeve (see page 73) – cut two. See note about size of grid squares on page 15.

Pattern for sleeve in two pieces (see page 73) – cut two

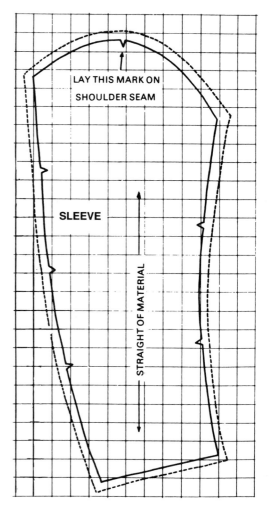

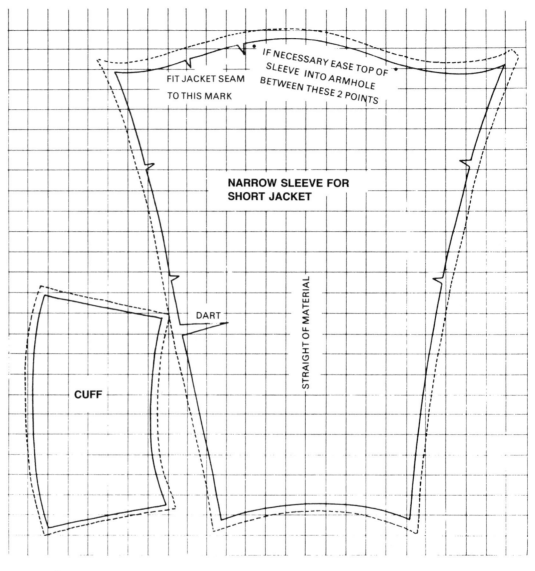

NARROW SLEEVE FOR SHORT JACKET

IF NECESSARY EASE TOP OF SLEEVE INTO ARMHOLE BETWEEN THESE 2 POINTS

FIT JACKET SEAM TO THIS MARK

DART

STRAIGHT OF MATERIAL

CUFF

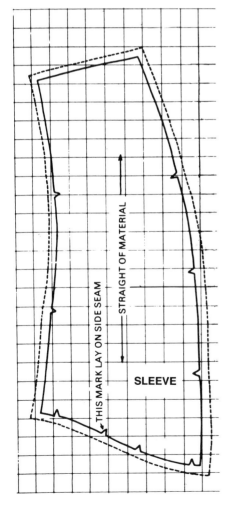

STRAIGHT OF MATERIAL

THIS MARK LAY ON SIDE SEAM

SLEEVE

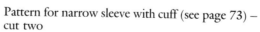

Pattern for narrow sleeve with cuff (see page 73) – cut two

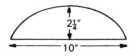

$2\frac{1}{4}''$

10″

Epaulette – cut two

Long tunic

Suitable materials

3¼–3½ yd (3m) of Bolton sheeting or strong cotton, velvet, velveteen, heavy satin, sateen, brocade (the tunic must be backed by firm calico or cotton in the same way as women's jackets, tutu bodices, etc.); strong hooks and eyes for fastening.

Method

1 Having measured and cut tunic, fit body firmly, allowing armhole to come as high up armpit and as low on shoulder as possible, but with arm swinging freely.

2 If sleeve is to be worn separately, cut another tunic (waist-length) in firm calico or cotton and hollow out neck. Fit firmly.

3 Machine darts at front and back. Press towards side seams.

4 Seam shoulders and side seams. Press.

5 If full sleeves and tunic are to appear slashed, stitch on pieces of material as indicated, padding and gathering these very slightly.

6 Seam sleeves. Gather full sleeve, or ease sleeve in two pieces. Set sleeve into armhole taking care that it rests exactly on edge of shoulder and well up into armhole.

Where sleeve is set on vest, it should be pulled about ¾ in. (2cm) higher than shoulder edge and below armpit. It is then stitched very firmly **over** vest.

7 Adjust hem of long tunic and sleeves on individual. Face both and also the neckline with piece of same material cut on cross.

Or adjust hem and sleeves of short tunic. Back piece of same material as tunic with firm calico and then face lower edge. Face sleeves and neck as in long tunic.

If cuff is required, cut as indicated in double material and back one side with tailor's canvas. Leave opening for fastening.

8 Turn in hem allowance, allowing good overlap at back. Stitch on strong hooks and eyes for fastening.

Where an épaulette is needed, cut in double material and back one side with tailor's canvas. Epaulette is then sewn on top of armhole of sleeveless tunic. Or it is finished off neatly and stitched firmly on to tunic after sleeves have been set. Similarly basque, or kilted piece, is sewn on after rest of tunic has been finished.

The basic leotard and additions

A large majority of costumes worn in the modern musical and in modern dance and ballet are based on a firm leotard made of silk or woollen jersey cloth, which is admirable for fitting the figure and showing off every line. On this base innumerable designs are made, some of which are indicated here.

It is important in cutting jersey cloth never to pull the material and always to cut the pattern 1 in. (2.5cm) less than the desired width when fitted as the jersey cloth stretches. Leotard will then fit closely to the figure. Also always use a loose tension when stitching.

The same pattern can be used for leotards in silks, satin, sateen, etc. These are never so successful as jersey, however.

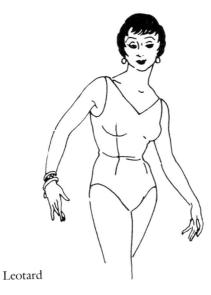

Leotard

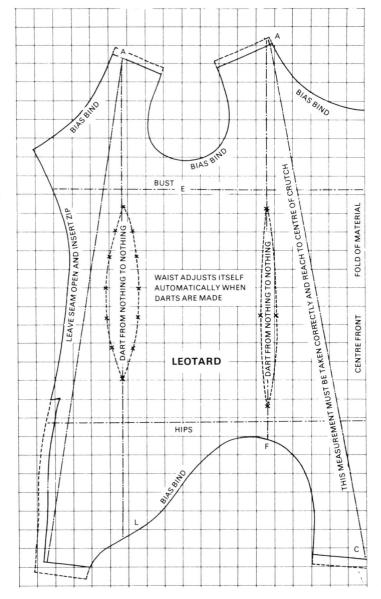

Materials required

Leotard only can be made out of ¾ yd (70cm) of silk, woollen or nylon jersey cloth which is usually 54 in. (140cm) wide and tubular. This length is ample for any size measuring 27in. (70cm) and less from **a** to crutch (see page 18). ¾ yd (70cm) can also be used for longer crutch measurements if an extra piece is sewn on crutch line as indicated. But this is not so satisfactory as the pattern cut in one piece.

Pattern for leotard. See note about size of grid squares on page 15.

Short full skirt

Method

1 Measure, cut and fit material. Dart under bust to roughly 3 in. (7.5cm) above lower edge front, and at back from bustline to roughly 4 in. (10cm) above lower edge back. (If leotard is topless make another dart directly under arm.)

2 Seam back from lower edge for 5–6 in. (12.5–15cm) depending on individual and insert zip. If this is not self-fastening a hook and eye must be added after top has been bound.

3 Seam crutch and shoulder seams. (If required.)

4 Cut strips of jersey cloth 1½ in. (4cm) wide on cross and bias bind all round neckline, armholes and leg (or if without shoulder pieces, all round top). Take care to pull this binding fairly tight as it holds the garment in place. (Cotton binding can also be used.)

ADDITIONS

Long straight skirt attached either to waist or hipline. This is merely two widths of jersey cloth seamed together and of requisite length from either waist to ankle or hip to ankle. These are hemmed at lower edge, turned over and gathered at top edge and sewn either at waist or hipline. Sew very firmly by hand.

Never machine a skirt to a leotard as the stitching quickly deteriorates.

Circular skirt attached to either waist or hipline. This is best made from some other soft material than jersey, which is inclined to drop and get out of shape when cut in this fashion. Make up as indicated. If an even fuller skirt is desired, add gores in places indicated by dotted lines. Or cut three pieces as indicated without hollowing out the waist segment so much. Then join three pieces together to make an extremely full skirt.

Short full skirt with or without basque. Cut short skirt as indicated in pattern and attach this to waist or hipline.

Or cut the basque on same lines as that for tutu, allowing this to come to point in front. Attach full circular skirt to this basque and then to waistline of leotard. Or it is often best to fasten such a skirt independently.

Sleeves cut to ½ or ¾ length can also be added. These are cut 1 in. (2.5cm) narrower than those in pattern for tight-sleeved jacket. They are set normally into armhole.

Soft draperies of the jersey cloth can be drawn over one shoulder or draped round hips. Similar draperies of net can be made. Short gathered net skirts can be added.

Cuffs, long gloves, bolero jackets and large collars can be worn for a Modern costume.

Circular skirt

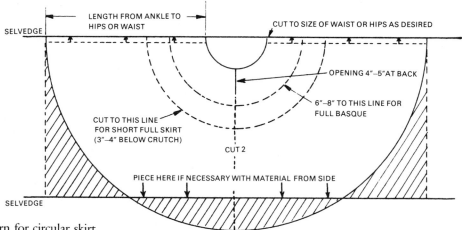

Pattern for circular skirt

National costume

National dancing is taking an increasing place in the syllabus of many schools and plays a large part in yearly displays and competitions. The following give some ideas of costumes which can be used, and with careful re-arrangements several different styles can be worked out by interchanging the patterns given.

In the making of National costume, aim first at giving the dancer the correct silhouette and shape of the garments. A good choice of material will then help these to hang properly. Most peasant costume is made of heavy materials with the exception of the very fine lawn blouses of the Balkans.

Colour in National costume is very important. The most usual colours are whites and creams, reds, oranges and blacks. Blues and greens in bulk are unusual and mauves and purples practically non-existent, and all these should only be used after careful reference to authentic costumes. It should be noted that most European countries are now issuing excellent series of postcards of authentic costumes which are correctly coloured. But care must be taken to distinguish between those postcards drawn with an eye to the fashion market, and those of the genuine folk costumes found in folk museums and art collections.

NATIONAL SKIRTS

Fully gathered

Traditionally used in Scandinavia, Holland, Italy, France and parts of central Europe.

Materials required
At least four widths of suitable material such as furnishing cotton, linen, heavy cotton, 36 in. (90cm) wide, measuring from waist to mid-calf plus 3 in. (8cm) for turnings, i.e. a 2-in. (5cm) hem is essential to give weight to the skirt and 1 in. (3cm) for double row of gathering and to set into waistband; piece of same material 3 in. (8cm) wide and long enough to go round waist of dancer for band. Strong hooks and eyes.

Method
1 Seam all four pieces together, leaving one seam open 7 in. (18cm) at top for placket.
2 Turn up hem allowance of 2 in. (5cm).
3 Make placket in ordinary way with false piece and hem.
4 Run two rows of gathering round top and set into waistband, arranging gathers evenly. Sew on hooks and eyes for fastening.

Pleated

Traditionally used in Poland, Hungary, Byelorussia, Czechoslovakia and Romania.

Materials required
At least four widths of suitable material as above, 36 in. (90cm) wide, measuring from waist to bottom of calf plus 3 in. (8cm) for turnings; piece of material 3 in. (8cm) wide and long enough to go round waist of dancer, or sufficient material to make short corselet (see page 86). Strong hooks and eyes.

Method
1 Seam all four pieces together leaving one seam open 7 in. (18cm) at top for placket.
2 Turn up hem allowance of 2 in. (5cm). Make placket in usual way.
3 Pleat material from top to hem, making pleats no more than 2 in. (5cm) wide, but adjusting these according to amount of material used. The more material used the more

Fully gathered skirt

Pleated skirt

deeply will the pleats fall under each other; in a Byelorussian skirt each pleat falls at least halfway under the next. Tack pleats, press and secure firmly together at the top.

4 Set top into waistband and sew on hooks and eyes for fastening.

Both gathered and pleated skirts in peasant costume are often set into the short corselet (page 86). This eliminates the untidy gaps between blouse and skirt which often occur when the dancer is in movement and is therefore admirable for classwork.

Circular skirt with frill

This was traditionally worn in urban areas round Moscow, Warsaw, Budapest, Prague, etc., and occasionally in Austria.

Materials required

At least 2½ yd (2.25m) of suitable material, as above, also satin or sateen. In this case, however, length is dependent upon length of skirt and amount of frill required.

If 36 in. (90cm) material is used, at least four widths are needed for frills. But five widths are the usual degree of fullness.

Method

1 Cut material according to pattern and seam side of skirt, leaving this open 7 in. (18cm) at top for placket. Or, if desired, waistline can be cut a little deeper, the top of the skirt set straight into a band and elastic threaded through.

2 Make usual placket at side-opening, set into waistband and sew on strong hooks and eyes.

3 Seam widths of frill together and hem lower edge.

4 Turn in and run two rows of gathering along top edge of frill. Adjust gathering evenly round lower edge of skirt and secure firmly. It is best to use two rows of machining.

NATIONAL BLOUSES

The true peasant blouse is actually part of the traditional basic shirt, which was at one time a knee-length dress. The following pattern with its four varieties of neckline and three types of sleeve is also used and is therefore of value for both classwork and shows.

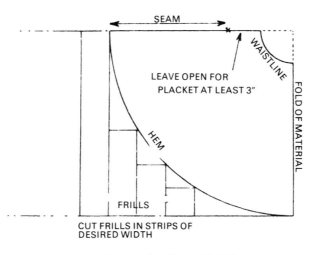

Pattern for skirt with frill

Circular skirt with frill

Short puff sleeves

Elbow-length sleeves

Full-length bishop sleeves

Short puff sleeves with a frilled edge and with a frilled and gathered neckline on a blouse traditionally worn in southern Germany, Austria, Switzerland and Italy. (Drawing is from the Black Forest.)

Elbow-length sleeves gathered into bands and with a gathered high neckline without frill on a blouse traditionally worn in Holland, Portugal (often with lace frills), Switzerland, Italy, Hungary, Russia, Czechoslovakia. (Drawing from Holland.)

Full-length bishop sleeves gathered at wrist with a frill and with a high neckline without frill on a blouse worn in Salzburg, Finland, Portugal, Spain, Sweden, Romania (sleeves also worn loose), Byelorussia, Italy, Germany, France. (Drawing from Spain.)

Materials required

2½ yd (2.3m) of fine linen, linen lawn, lawn, muslin or light cotton; 2 lengths of tape or elastic for neck and waist.

Method

1 Having measured and cut material, seam sides and shoulders.

2 For high or low *frilled* neckline, cut piece of material 3 in. (8cm) wide to same shape as neckline and face this. Run two rows of machining ¼ in. (5mm) apart round lower edge and thread in drawstring or elastic. For high or low neckline *without frill*, finish neck with bias binding and thread in drawstring.

3 Gather lower edge of sleeve and set into band which fits either upper arm for *short sleeve*; or just below elbow for ¾-*length*; or wrist for *long sleeve*. If sleeve is to be loose, turn up hem to length required. Gather upper end of sleeve and set into armhole.

4 3 in. (8cm) above lower edge, stitch on piece of bias binding for drawstring as blouse must be held firmly at waist. It is best to use tape for drawstrings as this does not perish with washing and makes the blouse easier to iron.

See note about size of grid squares on page 15.

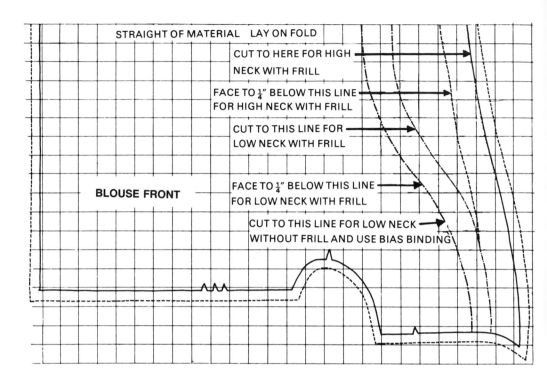

STRAIGHT OF MATERIAL   LAY ON FOLD

CUT TO HERE FOR HIGH NECK WITH FRILL

FACE TO ¼" BELOW THIS LINE FOR HIGH NECK WITH FRILL

CUT TO THIS LINE FOR LOW NECK WITH FRILL

BLOUSE FRONT

FACE TO ¼" BELOW THIS LINE FOR LOW NECK WITH FRILL

CUT TO THIS LINE FOR LOW NECK WITHOUT FRILL AND USE BIAS BINDING

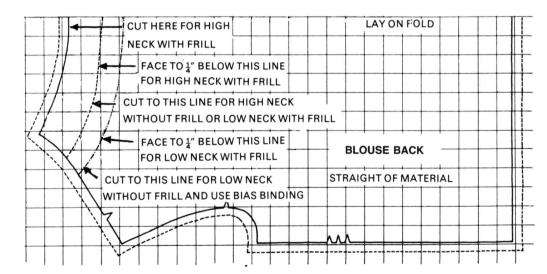

CUT HERE FOR HIGH NECK WITH FRILL

FACE TO ¼" BELOW THIS LINE FOR HIGH NECK WITH FRILL

CUT TO THIS LINE FOR HIGH NECK WITHOUT FRILL OR LOW NECK WITH FRILL

FACE TO ¼" BELOW THIS LINE FOR LOW NECK WITH FRILL

LAY ON FOLD

BLOUSE BACK

STRAIGHT OF MATERIAL

CUT TO THIS LINE FOR LOW NECK WITHOUT FRILL AND USE BIAS BINDING

Pattern for blouse.

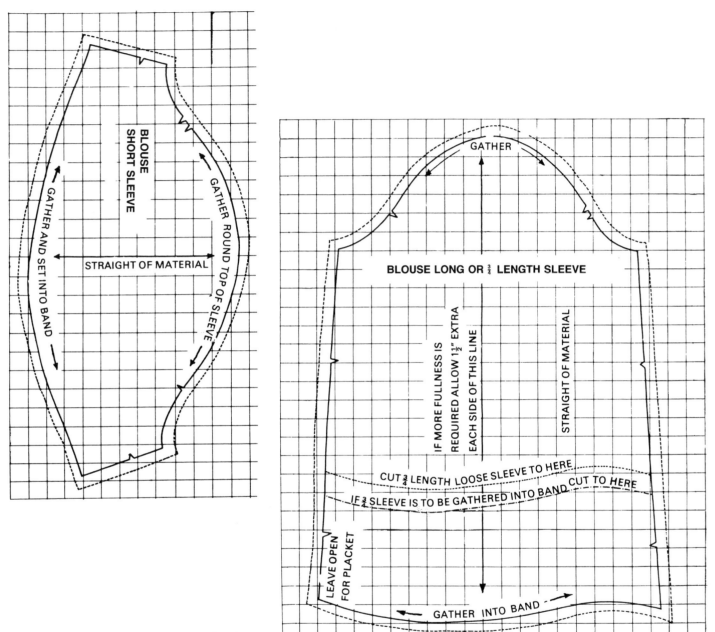

BLOUSE
SHORT SLEEVE

GATHER ROUND TOP OF SLEEVE

STRAIGHT OF MATERIAL

GATHER AND SET INTO BAND

GATHER

BLOUSE LONG OR ¾ LENGTH SLEEVE

IF MORE FULLNESS IS
REQUIRED ALLOW 1½" EXTRA
EACH SIDE OF THIS LINE

STRAIGHT OF MATERIAL

CUT ¾ LENGTH LOOSE SLEEVE TO HERE

IF ¾ SLEEVE IS TO BE GATHERED INTO BAND CUT TO HERE

LEAVE OPEN
FOR PLACKET

GATHER INTO BAND

Pattern for sleeves

Demi-caractère female dress

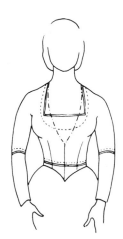

Diagram showing different neck, sleeve and waistlines

Numerous interesting costumes for the *demi-caractère* ballet can be made by designing appropriate additions to the longer-length ballet skirts. The following patterns and drawings are capable of other variations in addition to those suggested. It will be noted that many additions are based on items found in National costume, as the *demi-caractère* ballet is often a mixture of classical and character styles.

JACKETS WITH TIGHT-FITTING SLEEVES

Amongst the most attractive additions which can be made to the ballet skirt for *demi-caractère* work are tight-sleeved jackets with interesting necklines. These are based on traditional jackets worn by Greek, Bulgarian and Turk.

The pattern allows for three variations, but others could be made.

Materials required

3¼ yd (3m) velvet, velveteen, heavy silk or rayon, which must be backed by calico or firm cotton as in tutu bodice.

Method

1 Having measured and cut pattern and material, fit jacket very carefully. It should be firm with freedom allowed in the armholes, which should be cut as high into the armpits as possible.
2 Machine diagonal darts on fronts and straight darts at waist and shoulder back.
3 Seam fronts and back together at sides and shoulders. Seam sleeves together.

The square-necked, short-sleeved and short-waisted jacket of Holland, traditionally worn in Volendam

See note about size of grid squares on page 15

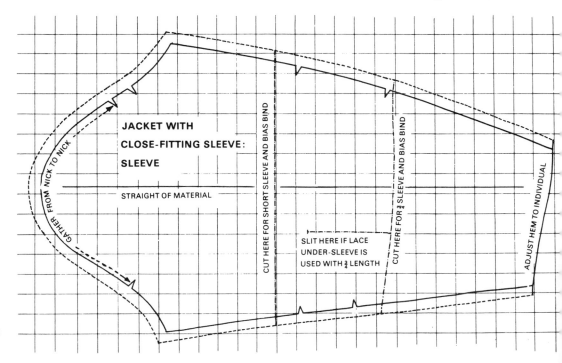

JACKET WITH
CLOSE-FITTING SLEEVE:
SLEEVE

GATHER FROM NICK TO NICK

STRAIGHT OF MATERIAL

CUT HERE FOR SHORT SLEEVE AND BIAS BIND

SLIT HERE IF LACE
UNDER-SLEEVE IS
USED WITH ¾ LENGTH

CUT HERE FOR ¾ SLEEVE AND BIAS BIND

ADJUST HEM TO INDIVIDUAL

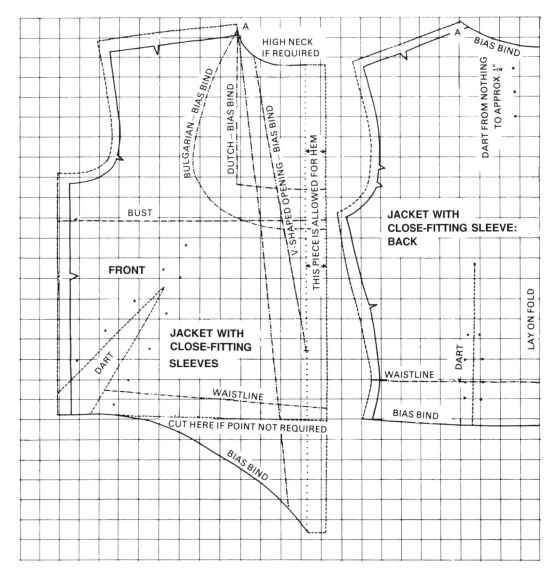

The V-necked pointed jacket with long or three-quarter length sleeves as worn in the Greek Amalia costume. If an épaulette were added, the suggestion would be made of a military costume.

The wide round-necked, short-sleeved and straight-waisted jacket of Bulgaria and Turkey. If a drapery were allowed to fall from it, the suggestion would be made of an Oriental costume.

4 Set sleeves into armholes and adjust to requisite length. Hem lower edge and, if slit is used, hem each side.

5 Turn in hem allowance at centre fronts for fastening.

6 Turn in hem allowance round neckline and lower edge. Face very firmly with piece of same material cut on cross.

7 Add whatever decoration is suitable for cut of jacket. Sew on strong hooks and eyes at front fastening.

THE CORSET OR CORSELET

The corset is a most important item of many *demi-caractère* and National costumes.

The pattern allows four variations, but others are possible. It is designed to be fastened at the front, but if it is to be used for *demi-caractère* work it is often better to make a back fastening, particularly if it is to become one with the rest of the costume. In this case, place centre front of pattern on fold

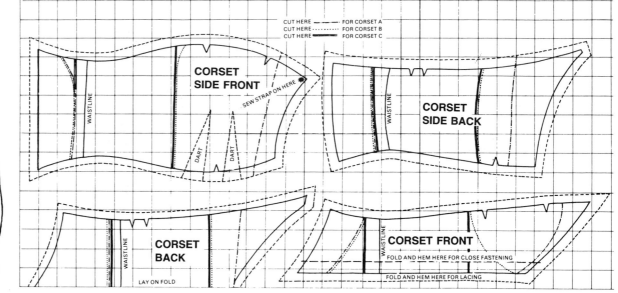

CUT HERE ——— FOR CORSET A
CUT HERE ·········· FOR CORSET B
CUT HERE ▬▬▬▬ FOR CORSET C

CORSET SIDE FRONT

SEW STRAP ON HERE

WAISTLINE

DART   DART

CORSET SIDE BACK

WAISTLINE

CORSET BACK

WAISTLINE

LAY ON FOLD

CORSET FRONT

WAISTLINE

FOLD AND HEM HERE FOR CLOSE FASTENING

FOLD AND HEM HERE FOR LACING

See note about size of grid squares on page 15.

A Full corset used in France, Norway, Austria, Finland, Germany, Spain, Czechoslovakia, Switzerland, Sweden, Italy. Drawing is from Poland.

B Heart-shaped corset used in Switzerland, Austria, Hungary, Czechoslovakia, Norway. Drawing is from Spain.

C High-fronted corselet used in France, Italy, Switzerland, Austria, Germany. Drawing is from Bavaria.

D Straight narrow corselet used in France, Italy and elsewhere. Drawing is from Sweden.

of material and centre back on selvedges, allowing at least 1 in. (2.5cm) extra for hem at centre back and fastening.

Materials required

1 yd (90cm) for full and heart-shaped corsets; ½ yd (45cm) for high-fronted and straight narrow corselets; velvet, velveteen, firm woollen cloth, which must be backed by calico or firm cotton as in tutu bodice.

Method

1 Having measured and cut material, fit corselet so that it clings firmly to the body.
2 Machine darts on side fronts. (These are not used in **C** and **D**.)
3 Seam side fronts and centre fronts together, being careful to keep material absolutely smooth. Snip raw edges before machining.
4 Seam side fronts and side backs together.
5 Turn in hem allowance round top and lower edge, mitring points when these occur. Face very firmly with piece of same material cut on cross.
6 Turn in hem allowance at centre fronts (or backs), allowing overlap if corselet is to be fastened by hooks or buttons; or a gap of 1½ in. (3.5cm) if corset is to be laced.
7 Sew on shoulder straps if required, to suit individual. Sew on strong hooks and eyes, or make buttonholes and sew on buttons for fastening. If corset is to be laced sew on largest eyes obtainable on both sides of opening. (Tiny curtain rings can also be used.) Use very strong narrow ribbon, braid or dyed string for lacing.

All corsets and corselets must be boned. With centre front opening, bones should be placed at each side of front and along side-back seams. With back opening, along side-front seams and side-back seams. Bones must fit to within ½ in. (1cm) of top and lower edge, and must be well padded at each end.

A low-necked, short-sleeved National blouse with heart-shaped corset, tiny apron and shorter ballet skirt

OTHER DEMI-CARACTÈRE ADDITIONS

Overskirt

An overskirt of ribbon or rug wool with cotton bobbles to suggest a Spanish (Goya period) or gipsy costume. Make a firm waist-belt of ribbon and attach about sixteen pieces of ribbon or thick rug wool from 10–12 in. (25–30cm) long. Catch these together lattice fashion as indicated and finish each end with bobbles of wool or cotton. These are easily made by winding wool round a circular card with a hole in the centre. The ends are then cut and tied securely.

Decorative overskirt

Upper arm sleeve

An upper arm sleeve of organdie or muslin. Make from a strip of material at least 16 in. (40cm) long and from 6–8 in. (15–20cm) wide. Join ends and hem on both sides. Run elastic through both hems. Such sleeves can give a peasant look when added to the longer skirt with a corset top.

Bolero

A bolero is often worn to suggest some Spanish, gipsy or Oriental costume. This requires careful fitting if it is to remain in place. A firmly fitting back, cut high in the neck, darted above the waist and with a shallow armhole is essential. The side seam then falls to the back of the armhole and allows the front of the bolero to fit and shape easily.

Materials required
¾ yd (70cm) velvet, felt, velveteen, Bolton sheeting, satin, sateen, firm linen

Method
1 Having measured and cut pattern and material, fit bolero and adjust length to requirements.

If material is thin it is often better at this point to cut another set of fronts and to machine front edges from shoulder to side

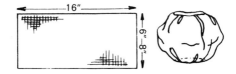

Upper arm sleeve

Bolero with decorative border

seam with right sides of material facing. Turn fronts right side out, tack round all edges and press. Machine two rows down front edges.
2 Machine darts at back. Seam sides and shoulders.
3 Face back of neck and lower edge of bolero with piece of same material 2 in. (5cm) wide cut on cross. Face armhole.

Or if fronts have not been lined as above, cut a long strip of material on cross 3 in. (8cm) wide and face outside edge of bolero: take care not to stretch front edges and ease facing inside at rounded corners of front.

See note about size of grid squares on page 15.

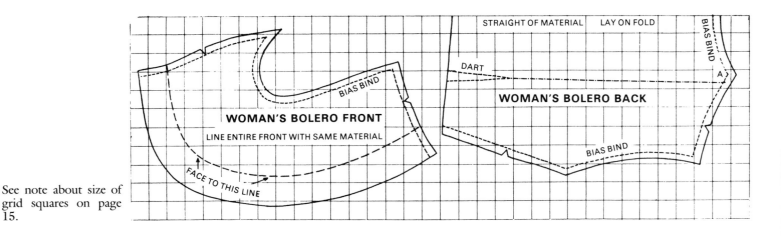

Bolero and ribbon attachment worn over shorter ballet skirt with lace head-dress

Carnival dress

Carnival ribbons

A *Swan Lake* length dress designed for a Masquerade or Carnival. Catch together on one shoulder five or six lengths of ribbon from 1–1½ in. (2.5–3.5cm) wide and ¾–1½ yd (70–140cm) long. Drape these across front of bodice and catch on opposite hip. Add some wool bobbles sewn on to varied lengths of wool or ribbon. Wire and cluster together a few short lengths of ribbon and mount on comb or net for a head-dress.

Demi-caractère male dress

The male *demi-caractère* costume can often be made by adding some item to either type of classical tunic. The illustrations suggest what can be done.

SHIRT AND BREECHES

The male basic shirt with loose sleeves and softly knotted tie is worn under a sash and knee breeches.

Breeches are made by cutting off the legs of tights below the knees. A design is then made from thick rug wool, stitched on as indicated.

THE SHORT TUNIC WITH FULL SLEEVES

The design suggested for the tunic can be made from odd pieces of material and stitched on with contrasting or self-coloured thread. Or the design can be outlined with rug wool stitched on with self-coloured thread.

This is worn with a half cape and sword belt. Cape is cut according to pattern and given a collar with pointed ends. This cape can be worn in various ways. If it is worn across the back do not use shoulder darts.

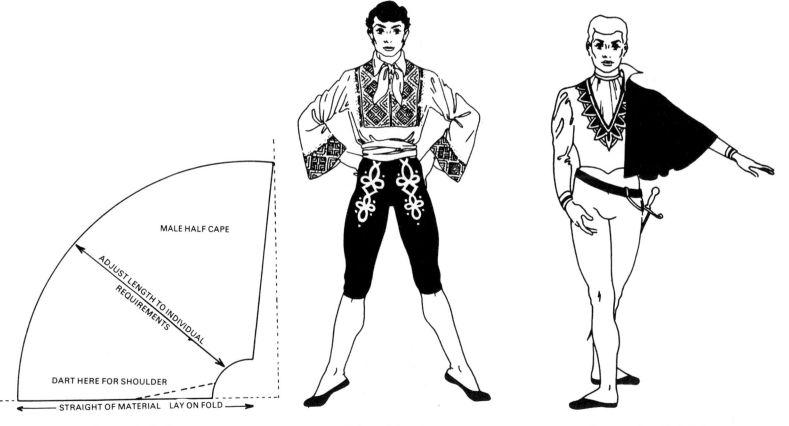

Pattern for half cape   Shirt and breeches   Short tunic with full sleeves

THE SHORT TUNIC WITH TIGHT SLEEVES

This is given a long basque slightly shaped to fit pointed front. Cuffs are added to the tight sleeves. A ruff for the neck and a sash are made from ribbon or material 12–18 in. (30–45cm) wide and 1–1½ yd (1–1.4m) long. The sash is draped over left shoulder and knotted on right hip.

THE LONGER TUNIC

The longer tunic with tight sleeves and centre fronts rounded at lower edge is given a border of fur and frogging. The fur edge is easily simulated by using a strip of coarse canvas knotted with rug wool. It is not necessary to knot the wool as closely as in rug-making. (A knot through every other hole is ample.) The frogging can similarly be imitated either with rug wool or cord, pinned to desired pattern and secured with strong thread. Similar frogging can be stitched to tights.

Short tunic with tight sleeves

Longer tunic with tight sleeves

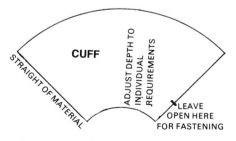

Pattern for cuff on short tunic with tight sleeves

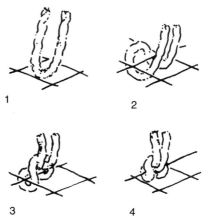

1   2

3   4

Diagram showing how to use rug wool

To knot wool

If a proper rug hook is not available, use a coarse crochet hook. Cut wool into 3 in. (8cm) lengths, fold one strand in half, thrust hook through canvas and pull doubled end through hole. Slip hook through loop thus made and pull loose ends through. Tighten knot.

BOOTS

These are often required in *demi-caractère* and character work. As they are extremely expensive to buy it is useful to make replicas of the upper part in felt. The following pattern only gives a basis for cutting an upper. The making of a shoe has to be far more precise than a costume, therefore ideal results can only be obtained after a certain amount of trial and error.

Materials required

½ yd (50cm) felt (if 60 in. (150cm) wide or over)

Method

1 Cut pieces to pattern, taking care to reverse pattern when cutting right foot, as boot is shaped to fit.
2 Stitch side seams of foot piece and seam at back of boot.
3 Snip edge of foot piece carefully round upper edge and turn in hem allowance. Stitch this edge over upper part of boot. Take care that centre front of foot piece meets centre front of upper, and centre back meets seam.
4 Stitch a strip of felt ½ in. (1.5cm) wide at edge of inner side seam. (Strip must be long enough to pass under instep to outer seam.) Slip completed upper on leg and then fit slipper (never try to push felt over slipper). Catch felt strip firmly on to outer seam. Strap must hold upper firmly.
5 Snip carefully all round lower edge of felt and glue to shoe. Overlap snips where necessary.

For high Polish or Hungarian boots, upper should be reinforced with tailor's canvas so that they stay up when in movement. For shorter boots the felt is usually stiff enough.

Pattern for boot (see note about size of grid squares on page 15)

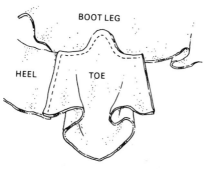

BOOT LEG

HEEL   TOE

Diagram of boot in making.

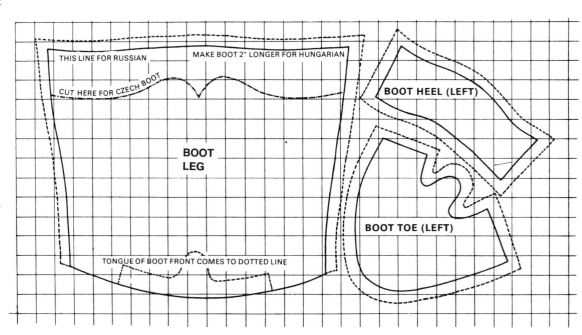

THIS LINE FOR RUSSIAN

CUT HERE FOR CZECH BOOT

MAKE BOOT 2" LONGER FOR HUNGARIAN

BOOT HEEL (LEFT)

BOOT
LEG

BOOT TOE (LEFT)

TONGUE OF BOOT FRONT COMES TO DOTTED LINE

Draperies

The fluttering draperies, so characteristic of many Russian productions, and which contribute such *brio* to their dancers' inimitable leaps, runs and turns, have become almost a fundamental badge of office comparable to the tutu. No doubt this costume was originally inspired by the numerous concerts given in Russia by Isadora Duncan and her neo-Greek dance recitals.

These costumes are usually deceptively simple and even casual in appearance. They are adapted with sleeves for *Juliet*, vine leaves for *Walpurgis Night*, etc., and appear in various lengths. Do not be beguiled into thinking they are 'easier to get away with' than a tutu, because they have a similar trick of showing up your faults rather than concealing them.

They are usually based on the circular skirt, split to the top of the thigh and made of soft voile, chiffon or man-made fibres which do not stick to the body. A well-fitted cotton bodice lines the top, on which the sheer material is draped in different ways. The edges are sealed with shellac rather than hemmed, to preserve maximum lightness.

Curtsey and bow

At the end of every class, just as at the end of every performance, pupils, students, *corps de ballet* and even the ballerina herself, together with her partner, the *danseur noble*, must curtsey or bow. In the classroom the pupils and students should acknowledge the efforts of the teacher who has given them a lesson. On stage, the dancers must acknowledge the applause of the audience, who have paid to see them dance and who are now rewarding the dancers for their efforts.

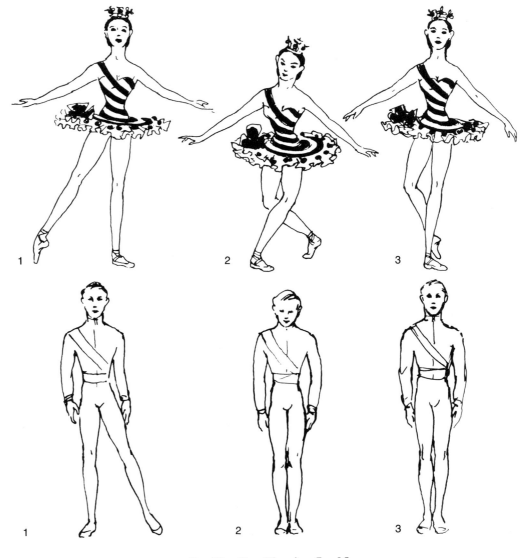

1 2 3

1 2 3

C U R T A I N

Index

This index has been organised with particular reference to the elucidation of French terms. If the reader encounters a term and wishes to know its meaning, a page number in **bold** given in this index will refer him to the place where he will find an explanation in English and the French verb relative to the term. For this purpose, the reader may also turn to page 37.